A Teacher's Stories

A Teacher's Stories

Reflections on High School Writers

Joyce Greenberg Lott

Boynton/Cook Publishers
HEINEMANN
Portsmouth, NH

Boynton/Cook Publishers, Inc.
A subsidiary of Reed Elsevier, Inc.
361 Hanover Street, Portsmouth, NH 03801-3912
Offices and agents throughout the world

Every effort has been made to contact the copyright holders and students
for permission to reprint borrowed material. We regret any oversights
that may have occurred and would be happy to rectify them in future
printings of this work.

Credits for previously published material begin on page 167.

Acquisitions Editor: Peter R. Stillman
Production Editor: Renée M. Pinard
Cover designer: Julie Hahn

Library of Congress Cataloging-in-Publication Data
Lott, Joyce Greenberg.
    A teacher's stories : reflections on high school writers / Joyce
  Greenberg Lott.
        p.   cm.
    Includes bibliographical references.
    ISBN 0–86709–331–5
    1. English language — Composition and exercises — Study and teaching
  (Secondary) — United States — Case studies.   2. Lott, Joyce
  Greenberg.   I. Title.
  LB1631.L53   1994
  808'.042'0712 — dc20   93–43816
                                                                      CIP

Printed in the United States of America on acid-free paper
98 97 96 95 94   BB   1 2 3 4 5 6 7 8 9

To my husband, Gary Lott,
and to my parents, Florence and David Feinstein,
without whose support this book would have been
impossible to write

Contents

Foreword

The Act of Reflection: In physics, a change of direction in which a ray of light, sound, or other form of radiant energy strikes upon a surface and is thrown back in to the same medium from which it approached.

To reflect: To bend or throw back; to give back an image or likeness to be mirrored; to think seriously, consider.

— Webster's Unabridged Dictionary

What is a teacher to do who finds herself, after a dozen classroom years, somehow disenchanted, haunted by seeming failures? Failure to Joyce Lott meant increasing dissatisfaction with the results of traditional tactics. Despite her meticulous evaluations, careful comments, and grading practices worthy of a Solomon, certain of Joyce's students still did not progress. Neither the quality nor the quantity of their work improved, let alone their love of writing, which this particular teacher (published herself in prose and poetry) was determined to amplify. Perplexed, Joyce watched as her painstaking comments numbed her students' self-esteem and motivation when she most meant to enhance them. Far from encouraging a new generation of writers, the tried-and-true methods at her disposal were alienating some of the writers who were enrolled in Joyce's courses.

Consequently, she began to question her own effectiveness, her very profession: "Maybe I'm not meant to be a teacher. I make too many mistakes." Fortunately, bonds to her pupils were sound enough to prevent a rash departure. Yet something had to be done for the sake of those on both sides of the desk. Joyce realized that she required reflection. She had to climb the mountain, to search for an overview, to find new pathways.

At first, sheer numbers and ethnic complexities, coupled with lack of private space for herself or for regular conferences, seemed to doom reflection. In desperation, Joyce turned to her lifetime ally: writing. She began to keep a running journal with rigorous notes on each school day, particularly on her own response to student reactions to grades and comments. Joyce forced herself to scrutinize tough issues like gender roles and cultural clashes, which she had to admit were getting in the way of student productivity and distorting her ability to be fully effective in response to high school writers. In fact, in three of her stories Joyce addresses "color blindness" and the new definitions she discovered within herself.

Recording her observations each evening on her computer for a year, Joyce compiled a prodigious file of primary source material. Journal-keeping immediately expanded Joyce's role into that of teacher/researcher. The initial effect on her was a welcome renewal of energy and enthusiasm for the task of teaching more than a hundred high school juniors and seniors. The process became self-sustaining: synchronistic books and conversations and professional conferences, all of which addressed the dilemma. Joyce began to solicit opinions on these issues from other educators who were committed to maintaining enthusiasm in young people whose creativity they must critique and foster. Back in her classroom, Joyce began to look upon her charges as her richest resource. She built new bridges of trust. Ultimately, Joyce and her students became explorers together in new territories.

Joyce developed a portfolio program, a precise contract for those who studied with her in which she set firm limits but removed the specter of teacher-as-judge until the end of each marking period. In the interim, students could choose which work to revise and which to exclude or include in the final portfolio. Papers could change form, such as from prose to poetry. Joyce had offered her classes a time of reflection.

Most students thrived in the new environment, so much so that Joyce was criticized by a colleague for "grading too high." Her thesis remains, however, that when "students are given the opportunity to revise and reflect [in a supportive atmosphere], their writing will improve and so will their grades." For six months during her sabbatical Joyce Lott turned a relentless lens upon what was and was not working in that classroom. The result: *A Teacher's Stories*.

In her own reflection process, Joyce fully learned as much as her students, encapsulating her lessons in lines of stark honesty: "I traveled from what I knew into what I did not know," and "Teaching is not about proving you're right."

I have been a friend of Joyce's since the 1970s. As friend and peer, I looked forward to discovering new approaches when Joyce's manuscript for *A Teacher's Stories* was finally ready to share. Unexpectedly, I was often moved to tears and laughter. Her affection for her students, coupled with her frank self-examination and her no-nonsense writing skills, really brings these students to life. I admire Joyce's courage in facing these issues privately, let alone setting them under the electron microscope of sabbatical attention. I am doubly impressed now that her fellow teachers — as well as her students and their parents — can read her dilemmas.

Joyce is quick to point out that this work is not prescriptive, yet there is willingness to risk in *A Teacher's Stories*. What Joyce has done here for herself and others is to insist upon the right, the courage to begin again. This book is nothing less than the story of the transformation of a teacher. But the process does not stop at Joyce Lott's desk. Nor are the lessons limited to the classroom. Let the stories speak for themselves.

CAROLYN FOOTE EDELMANN

Acknowledgments

My thanks to the South Brunswick School District for supporting me during my half-year sabbatical and for giving me time to reflect. Thanks also to Barbara King-Shaver, my department supervisor, for encouraging me and for commenting on an early draft of the portion headed "The Setting."

My appreciation to all my students for putting up with my frustrations and enthusiasms. If it were not for them, I would have no stories. Special thanks go to Christina Borbeley, Jason Bullard, Heather Buten, Brendan Carroll, Christopher Cenkner, Amy Conover, Kimberly Halas, Kevin Julius, William Lee, Michael Leung, Amy Lisco, Robert Patey, Jonathan Philips, Kimberly Ritter, Kristen Spannagel, Sirinivas Tatini, Suzanne Tiedemann, Erika Troke, Carla Wingo, and William Wolff for granting me permission to tell their stories to others.

I would never have been able to write these stories if it were not for the support of family and friends. Each morning my cat, Clive, awaited my arrival, lying patiently on the rug in front of my desk as I procrastinated. Each afternoon my husband, Gary, came home from his own job as a high school history teacher, cheerfully carrying in the groceries and inquiring about my progress. Many a night, after I had shown Gary what I had accomplished, we argued over philosophy and language. His reactions helped me to see my work more clearly.

My husband and I are not the only family members who are teachers. My daughter, Suzanne Greenberg, and her husband, Michael Smith, are both teachers and writers. Each of them read my manuscript in progress, advised me how to order it, and gave me caring and helpful comments.

My friends have been equally generous. Meredith Knowlton, Connie Myslik, Penelope Schott, and Mimi Schwartz listened to my ideas, gave me suggestions when I asked for them, and acted as careful readers. A special thanks goes to Carolyn Edelmann for her encouragement and for the informative foreword that she volunteered.

In addition, I am grateful to Peter Stillman, my editor at Boynton/Cook Heinemann, who replied to my proposal for *A Teacher's Stories* by telling me that my work was complex and thoughtful, giving me the courage to continue writing. Last but not least, my special gratitude to Renée M. Pinard, who believed in me enough to organize my unpolished thoughts.

Preface

*A*fter ten years of teaching English at South Brunswick High School, I was dissatisfied. Some of my students were progressing; others were not. I was also tired of spending my weekends commenting on student papers and watching my students glance only at their grades on Monday morning. Those who were disappointed with my judgment crumpled up my comments and threw their papers into the trash. What's more, I knew how those students felt.

The previous summer, I had been asked to contribute an essay to a book edited by Mimi Schwartz, *Writer's Craft, Teacher's Art: Teaching What We Know*. In her role as editor, Mimi passed my essay, along with essays from other contributors, around for comments. Although this procedure ultimately proved helpful, upon receiving my work with words crossed out and strong remarks in the margins, I felt vulnerable, inadequate, and angry. These emotions were connected to my insecurity: compared to established writers like Lynn Bloom, Richard Marius, and Kim Stafford, I wasn't sure that my own writing was "good enough." It didn't take me long to figure out that my students must often feel the same.

Realizing that the traditional method of commenting on finished papers did not ensure progress, I began to experiment by requiring one revision per marking period from my students *after* I commented on their writing. Also, I tried to make my comments more helpful by affirming and questioning rather than editing, labeling, or imposing my own style. Still, this was not enough. Some of my students were not advancing.

Anxious to figure out why, I decided to follow closely the work of diverse students from two of my senior academic English classes. Although seniors who planned to attend college signed up for these classes, Academic English IV was not considered to be of the highest academic caliber. Those with low skills were placed in A-level classes and those with high skills were recommended for honors. English IV and Academic English IV were a matter of choice, along with Journeys, an untracked, interdisciplinary cross-cultural elective. Very often students who thought academic classes were for nerds or who did not have a strong self-image signed up for English IV; risk-takers and those who were disenchanted with traditional learning often signed up for Journeys. Those who elected Academic English IV covered a wide range — from students who weren't college material, although their parents hoped otherwise, to the class valedictorian who was taking so many advanced placement courses that he wanted to coast.

My intention was to explore the effect of teacher comments on the papers of as wide a range — in terms of writing ability, gender, and background — of these college preparatory students as possible in an attempt to observe their progress. Since I had not known most of the students previously, I judged their writing ability on the basis of the quality of work they had handed in at the beginning of the year. Not having access to biographical histories, I defined background by what students told me about their past schooling. Continuing my research over three marking periods, I studied the impact that my responses had on students' revisions by keeping a record of my interaction with these students.

While I was collecting data and keeping a running journal on my home computer, I was still teaching five English classes and bringing home about fifty papers a week. For the first time, however, I saw myself as a teacher/researcher, not just a teacher. In this new role, two things happened. Outside the classroom, I became more focused: what I needed to learn began to appear before my eyes. Books I just happened to pick up either gave me answers or articulated questions that I had been unable to form. Conferences I attended introduced me to people whose ideas enlarged my own thoughts. Conversations with friends sent me running to my notebook to jot down phrases.

Within the classroom, I found that I listened to students more carefully than I had in my previous role as overworked English teacher. I also found myself looking more deeply into students' faces. Although I had always thought of students as individuals, I began to see their singularity even more sharply. No longer able to treat my classes as homogeneous masses defined by grade level, I became more aware of individual needs. What Dixie Goswami suggested might happen when she trained teacher/researchers at Breadloaf happened to me: I underwent a transformation.

Although I had paid lip service to individual differences before, it was not until I began collecting the material for these stories that I realized how differently Jennifer, leery of adults, and Jane, who saw herself *as* an adult, responded to my conferencing techniques, or how dissimilarly Rahul, whose parents came from India, and Joseph, so recently emigrated from Hong Kong, reacted in class due to their lack of familiarity with American culture.

By seeing my students as complicated individuals, my interactions with them became more difficult. Some days I felt as though I had overstepped my territory by becoming emotionally involved with them. For me, though, there was no way around this dilemma: writing and responding to literature have always been emotional activities. However, my students helped me. They taught me that teachers as well as students are people, that teachers can have an "attitude," too. Teachers and students play roles to mask our insecurities. Until I felt secure or frustrated enough to drop my one-dimensional role as English teacher with some of my students, their writing did not improve. They needed to trust me before they would risk communicating truly on paper.

During the course of this study, I did learn more about the teaching of writing. As I analyzed my interactions with these students, my mistakes became apparent and my approaches changed. For example, my discomfort with grading papers individually led me to change my method of assessment. Although requiring one revision a marking period had been a start, it no longer seemed sufficient. Furthermore, I realized the importance of cross-cultural literature within the English classroom. Pretending that all seniors are motivated by the same material was no longer possible.

Although much of what I learned was already established knowledge, in the hectic environment of a public high school, I had not had sufficient time or distance to fully see and digest what other professionals were doing. This led me to request a sabbatical, the first given in our high school in many years, which was granted for a half-year the following spring.

During the fall semester before my sabbatical I made the decision to use portfolios in my classroom. Although evaluating portfolios is not a new idea, it was new to my school. Everything I had read about them appealed to my developing philosophy of the teaching of writing. Not only could students choose the work they wanted to present, but they would also have the opportunity to continue to revise. More and more I became aware of the importance of involvement, time, and reflection in the writing process. Since students arranged their own portfolios and selected the contents, it was impossible for them to remain uninvolved. And by reflecting on their writing-in-process, they were forced to grow and change. In allowing students a greater degree of involvement and also sufficient time to get comments from different people at various stages of their work, I hoped that more of my class would be inspired to think of themselves as writers. So, for that fall semester, I required portfolios from my students to be handed in each marking period. Excerpts from these portfolios, along with a description of the portfolio process, are included in Part Five of this book.

During my sabbatical, I appreciated having time to read books and attend workshops, but I learned the most through silent contemplation, trying to recreate student interactions as completely as possible. As these stories revealed themselves, I began to understand that knowing who my students were as people not only affected my interaction with them, it also affected their writing and whether it progressed or not.

A response that was successful with one student could be destructive with the next. An interaction that motivated one student to progress sometimes induced another to regress. That is why these stories focus on individuals. While analyzing one student's academic success, I found it necessary to consider her self-confidence. As I wrote about another's lack of progress, I found I needed to discuss his personal goals. I could not observe the effect of my response on a student's writing without observing how my personality affected that student. Before long, I began to wish that adolescent development, along with curriculum, was discussed more frequently among teachers at the high school level. I also began to wish that teacher training included case studies so that teachers could have the opportunity to examine and analyze human interaction earlier.

This book sets up issues we all deal with in one way or another. Ben Nelms articulated some of the questions I wanted to answer in his introduction to my first published case study, "Jeremy: Sex, Lies, and Masks," in the March 1991 issue of *English Journal*. "As English teachers, we often 'replay' critical classroom incidents in our minds," Nelms wrote. "'How well did I handle this situation?' we ask ourselves. 'What happened, and why did it happen, and how could I have improved my performance or my student's performance?' 'What can I learn from this experience that will enter into my decision-making in the future?'" To answer these questions for myself and to open this discussion for others, I have committed these stories to writing.

"Why don't our high school students write better?" ask so many adults in America. Teachers' stories are steps toward answering that question. Too often outsiders judge our teachers and schools in a vacuum, assuming a notion of development that is linear, particularly in the area of teaching writing. This book attempts to recreate what actually happens, to fill the vacuum with real people. It depicts the hard work of the writing classroom with its successes, failures, and sometimes frustrating lack of resolution.

Certainly, in the teenage world of TVs, telephones, and compact discs, the written word may not be valued, but many of us continue to recognize its importance. In pursuance of teaching students to write better, I offer the following stories as vehicles that may in some way help.

Introduction

The Setting

As with most stories, these stories have a setting—within the context of South Brunswick, a sprawling township in central New Jersey that covers forty square miles. Sandwiched between Route 130 and the turnpike to the east and rambling over both sides of Route 1 to the west, South Brunswick has an elusive geographical identity: it's in-between. No town exists, nor is there a town center. Some kids hang out at the Kendall Park Roller Rink or at the recreation complex on New Road. Others wait at the Suburban Transit bus stop to escape to Princeton to the south or New Brunswick to the north. But very few take the hour bus ride all the way north to New York City. "The City's too dangerous and too expensive," they tell me.

Much of South Brunswick used to be farmland. Until a few years ago, we still had a special program in the schools for children of migrant workers. Now, extra laborers aren't needed to pick beans and tomatoes; farmland has been replaced by housing. And each development presents its own socioeconomic picture—Kendall Park with its thirty-five-year-old shingled ranches, Dayton Square with its brand new townhouses; Brunswick Acres with its four- and five-bedroom colonials and split levels; and, on the other side of Route 1, the Monmouth Junction Trailer Park, which is so large I got lost in it driving a student home.

South Brunswick's population lives in condominiums and works in offices along the Route 1 corridor, commutes from three hundred thousand dollar houses to businesses in New York City, and rents homes where old vehicles clutter the driveway. The population includes bankers, stockbrokers, shopkeepers, professors, scientists, technicians, truck drivers, and day laborers. About eighteen thousand people live in South Brunswick — and more keep coming. Many people have been in the township for several generations; some have moved recently from places as distant as Thailand or Pakistan.

The township itself has crises of identity. And the decreasing percentage of its residents who share a common history makes achieving a sense of community even more difficult. In order to engender community, South Brunswick has established new traditions, made old ones more elaborate, and begun to provide for special needs. Often these activities, like Community Unity Day and Fourth of July celebrations, have taken place on our high school's football field. Just recently, a social center for senior citizens was dedicated in the back of the municipal building.

Like the township, our schools are also changing. It was not surprising that the theme of this year's full faculty meeting was "change," or that the keynote speaker's theme was "Creating a Climate for Change." One of our first superintendents began his career by taking potential dropouts fishing. In many ways, he symbolized the district's independent, rugged, and caring attitude. The superintendent who replaced him resigned after reforming the budget process, implementing site-based management, and integrating technology into instructional programs. Although he was competent, the Board questioned his style of leadership.

South Brunswick High School itself continues to change rapidly, and not without trauma. For the first time we have required seniors in Advanced Placement (AP) English to take the AP Exam. In previous years, seven or fewer students out of forty or more voluntarily did this. Some of our teachers have taught at South Brunswick from its incipiency; a few have graduated from the high school themselves; and others, like myself, have come from the outside. All of us, though, have had to keep up with the changes that have taken place.

The high school, which at this point is overcrowded, is a long, low building of nondescript color with a partial second story. More than a half-dozen years ago, it was expanded to include a new gym and library, as well as new industrial arts classrooms and offices. Just a few years ago, we celebrated the original building's twenty-fifth anniversary. Behind the high school is a parking lot for seniors, and beyond that lie two trailers, home of Project Promise, South Brunswick High School's award-winning alternative program. Project Promise was created to help students who were not successful within the structure of a large school. To the left of the trailers is the football field with its perimeter used for outdoor track. Behind the stadium are tennis courts, and beyond the courts is Crossroads, South Brunswick's middle school. That is also where the high school's auto shop is housed.

Inside South Brunswick High School's elongated building are locker-lined corridors labeled A, B, C, and D. Four minutes are allowed to move through the corridors between classes, with an extra minute permissible for students coming from the gym or shops in the new wing. A piercing bell sounds before and after each four-minute period, and hall monitors check students for properly signed slips if they are in the hall during classes.

Two hundred and thirty-seven seniors graduated in 1993. Of this number, slightly more than half planned to attend a four-year college. The greater percentage of these students continued their education in New Jersey. Another quarter planned to attend a two-year school, in most cases Middlesex County Community College, while they also would work to earn money for car insurance payments and other items they considered necessities. Of the graduating class of 1993, the remaining 21.9 percent had already achieved full-time employment. Many found jobs through the school's senior work/study program; 1.7 percent joined the military, and 5.9 percent planned to attend a career school.

This class of seniors came from diverse circumstances: intact families, single-parent homes, and foster homes. Many were born in the township; a few arrived here just months before graduation. Our student body speaks thirty-five languages, ten or eleven of which are Indian dialects. Although many of the newcomers are Indian or Asian, we are also getting a growing number of Hispanics. Of every size, shape, and color, and featuring every possible hairdo, these seniors are impossible to stereotype.

Many need support and supervised activities beyond the classroom. South Brunswick provides this for them by offering the services of six guidance counselors, two school nurses, one full-time therapist, two part-time therapists, a drug and alcohol counselor, and a special education department. Most recently, a competitive grant process highlighting our existing human services approach connected us to the College of Medicine and Dentistry of the State University of New Jersey in delivering family-based counseling in our school. We also staff a teen center that operates during the summer and as part of our school year co-curricular program. Juniors have a special opportunity to participate in an experiential learning program where they do supervised work in the community one day a week.

The United States Department of Education selected us for national recognition as a Blue Ribbon School in 1990–91 because of the many programs we have for students of different abilities and interests. Proud to lead a Blue Ribbon School and anxious to promote a spirit of pride among teachers and students, Richard Kaye, our principal, hosted a Blue Ribbon Bash and ordered pins for all staff members and three thousand bumper stickers for the community. At times our high school community seems like a big family.

If South Brunswick High School is an extended family, the English department is a nuclear one. Some of its thirteen members have been teaching together so long that they share not only professional concerns but personal ones as well. Much like a counseling support group, the members stick together throughout the day.

Similar to the rest of the district, our department is going through change, which is not easy for everyone. When I joined the English department, eleven of the twelve members were women and the supervisor was a man. Even though his stance was autocratic, teachers actually had great freedom. Curriculum was fairly loose and specified only in terms of available books in the bookroom. Although few of these books were written by minorities or women, we could pretty much do what we wanted with the materials we had. The negative aspect of this style of leadership was that it led to little continuity in curriculum. On the positive side, teachers did some exciting work behind classroom doors.

As far as writing instruction went, both the chair and several department members had been trained in the New Jersey Writing Project, begun at Rutgers University in 1977 and modeled after the Bay Area Writing Project in California. Teachers trained in the New Jersey Writing Project experienced, through writing and participation in a writing workshop, that writing was a process that covered five stages: prewriting, writing/drafting, revising, editing, and postwriting. In the prewriting stage, writers discovered their material, selected a subject, considered purpose and audience, and gathered information. While drafting, they developed their material and put it into a logical order. During revision, content and organization were changed, or content was rearranged, supplemented, or deleted. Editing, which usually followed rather than preceded revision, was the stage in which writing was evaluated for style, word choice, sentence structure, grammar, usage, spelling, and mechanics. Finally, postwriting involved going public with the work—giving it to an instructor for evaluation, reading it aloud, or publishing it in the workshop.

Peers and the instructor also commented on participants' writing at several stages as part of this process. And although the five events in the writing process were discussed in a linear manner, the process itself was actually experienced as recursive. Participating writers constantly moved back and forth to reevaluate and adjust their work, to review what they had written, and to plan the next step.

But, as sometimes happens, this process became simplified and institutionalized through the years within our department.

No longer experienced as recursive, writing as taught at South Brunswick High School came to be a lockstep action that included — almost always in the same order and with little variation — a rough draft, peer editing, and a final copy that was evaluated and commented on by the teacher. Although well-intentioned, most teachers studiously followed the linear steps of what, like a game of whisper-down-the-lane or telephone, was passed on as the writing process.

Several years ago, department members became concerned that students were not having the experience of working with a sufficient variety of writing modes before graduation and agreed to teach a formulaic approach to writing using an Interact program called STEPS. Brought to the department by the assistant superintendent in charge of curriculum and piloted by a teacher in the English department, STEPS forced students to organize and support their ideas. Although the program was controversial within the department as a whole, it particularly appealed to more traditional members.

Upon his retirement a few years ago, our supervisor was replaced by a woman who had earned a doctorate at Rutgers Graduate School of Education. She and I saw mostly eye to eye since we held similar educational philosophies, but she had the difficult job of pulling together a disparate department. To this purpose, she held long meetings every Monday after school and again for a week over the summer to tighten up and reorganize curriculum.

Since it is constructed by all members of a department, curriculum at South Brunswick is not handed down from the top. Moreover, changes are made periodically. According to South Brunswick's philosophy, curriculum is always in process. In reality, this process is often limited by three factors: disagreement among a department's members, available money for new materials, and energy within a department. Our new supervisor is a woman of great energy and also had administrative support. As a result, we purchased multicultural anthologies that included world literature and women and minority writers. Since my research took place a year before this change, readers will see that switching to this curriculum for juniors and seniors was an answer to direct and indirect student demands.

Because we were reorganizing the curriculum, our department head also asked us to articulate just what writing skills should be taught at each grade level, by identifying a writing core so that students not only had experience with a variety of writing modes before graduation, but were also prepared for the New Jersey High School Proficiency Test. Although the core must be covered, in theory there is flexibility: how and when the core is taught during the year is up to the classroom teacher. Also, the teacher can add works outside the core, provided they are not covered in other grades. In practice, however, many teachers are not anxious to teach more than the core. In other words, most teachers don't have time to grade more than required papers. Therefore, rather than encouraging writing development in a variety of discourse modes, many teachers have ended up limiting writing to particular matrices.

Depending on their ability grouping, freshmen are required to write an intermediate or advanced expository essay as defined by the formulaic models in STEPS from both a personal and literary viewpoint. Sophomores are to write persuasive, comparison/contrast, and problem-solving essays at the basic, intermediate, and advanced levels with the latter two essays to be formatted according to STEPS. And juniors are to write a cause-and-effect essay and expand on the other forms of essay writing that have already been taught previously.

Although our supervisor (with some department support) has been trying to move away from a formula-based program to one that is model based and trying to reinstate the practice of a more recursive writing process, a few department members who have done little writing themselves are fearful. Anxious to be told exactly what to teach, they have not considered Janet Emig's philosophy that writing is predominantly learned rather than taught. Even so, those of us who are less timid still ask the big questions: Should essay forms be taught at all? When do students learn forms? How do students learn them? Should teachers model for students? Do students learn by reading other essays? Do students discover forms themselves?

Since we work in a district in which we cannot assume that students have had experience engaging in descriptive or persuasive tasks that might prepare them for the more formal tasks they will encounter in the later grades, we worry about what to emphasize. Often, we go overboard by not asking students to tell stories or to play with language in tentative, exploratory ways in order to inform their more formal language tasks.

Apart from the fact that a formula-based approach to writing is alien to my nature (one of my colleagues calls STEPS a recipe book), learning to write formulaically creates two problems that are clearly visible at the senior level: First, students become more interested in following forms than in being creatively invested in their own work, and second, they come to think of writing as an activity similar to coloring in a coloring book that requires little thinking. Philosophically, I prefer to encourage exploration and development of students' abilities and interests rather than teach rhetorical patterns. This puts me in a peculiar position within the department.

Not only is our department now divided about how to teach writing, with the greater number of teachers being traditionalists, but also most dialogue on this topic ends up as an argument. Upper-grade teachers blame lower-grade teachers for "unprepared students." The usual scapegoat, however, is the middle school. Frustrated with their students' skill level and needing a target, department members bellow biweekly, "Middle school teachers don't teach a thing! All they do is pat kids on the head and tell them they're writers. No wonder our students don't believe us when we tell them they're not." Clearly, communication needs to be strengthened between the middle school and high school. At a recent department meeting, at least fifteen minutes was spent arguing about the description of the tracking system at the middle school; no one had exact information about how our students had been tracked.

Fury, frustration, and depression surface periodically in our department. Teachers are defeated by the level at which they find their students, by the wide range of ability within their classrooms, and by the size of their course loads. Recently, when these frustrations were expressed to the administration, the reply was "You chose to teach public school. What did you expect?"

Sometimes at department meetings, I find it hard to breathe, but when students are in the office, the atmosphere lightens.

At the time of the writing of the following stories, these were my working conditions. The twelfth-grade Minimum Core Proficiencies in Writing looked like this:

Writing

By the end of twelfth grade students in English 12 will be able to write all the forms studied in grades 9–11 and the following:
an autobiographical sketch
an advanced persuasive essay
a contrast critical analysis essay
an advanced literary or film analysis essay
two poems whose form is determined by literary models
a work whose form is based on a model read (such as *Metamorphosis*)
Students will be able to revise and edit the above for content, organization, grammar, usage and mechanics.

All department members teach English; we have no separate writing courses, although I wish we did. Most writing assignments are literature based and connected to the text that the class is then studying. In many cases, English teachers assign an essay as a way to complete a unit and assess what students have learned. A problem with this approach is that in the course of a school year, students write more essays than they read; another problem is that teachers carry home large stacks of papers to grade on a regular basis. Although this paper grading is burdensome to teachers and discouraging to students—often hindering students from experimenting and growing as writers—English teachers perpetuate the system in order to compile grades for interim notices, marking period reports, and final averages.

A full teaching load consists of five courses (all of which meet five days a week), a preparation period, and a duty period. For several years, instead of sitting in the hall or proctoring study halls, some of us have pulled "writing lab duty." Since we don't have a real writing lab, lab duty means we get to sit in the English office and either wait for our students (or someone else's) to walk in, tutor an assigned student who is having trouble passing a state test, or make an appointment to work with a particular person. This is the writing lab I refer to in the text.

Academic English IV

That brings me to my classroom and my curriculum. The immediate setting for these stories was C102, a room with no windows, two doors, blackboards on two walls, corkboard on the third, and file cabinets and a closet along the fourth wall. In C102, I taught Academic English IV seniors first period in the morning and last period in the afternoon. The remainder of the day, I was assigned elsewhere and C102 was assigned to other teachers. At South Brunswick, we don't have our own classrooms where we can arrange chairs, tables, and supplies. Scheduling and a shortage of space preclude this.

Although Academic English IV has an impressive title, its content at the time of these stories was a potpourri. Several years before, seniors had chosen an elective each semester. With the establishment of academic and regular classifications and because of budgeting and book availability, some of the contents of these electives were transferred. Film, one of the most popular offerings, was combined with the twelfth grade curriculum. In this elective, *The Graduate* had been used to teach film analysis. Students learned to discuss framing, placement, camera distance and angle, arrangement, lighting, color, sound, and movement while watching this film. Thus, many references are made to it in my stories.

Due to the penchant of our former department head, we taught many plays. Tennessee Williams's *A Streetcar Named Desire,* to which I also allude frequently, was among them. Although some of the other materials I refer to are more traditional in nature, a few were used only because of availability. At this point, our curriculum is no longer such a potpourri: we now teach world literature senior year.

By the time they progressed to twelfth grade, several students still confused *their* and *they're;* most did not understand subjective and objective pronouns, let alone agreement; and only one or two were sure of the difference between *lie* and *lay.* Those who had been through our program did know that an essay had an introduction, a body, and a conclusion, and some had learned about support. Some newcomers to the school, though, knew nothing about organization.

Although what I am describing sounds like a very conventional approach to composition, it satisfied most of the department members. They saw their job as teaching students to write organized essays in which ideas were expressed clearly and connected by transitions and that contained few technical errors.

Often, the only knowledge that most seniors held in common was that writing was not enjoyable. The general climate in C-hall was that English teachers hated to read papers and students hated to write them. That bothered me. Sitting at my desk in room C102, I yearned to open a window to gain new perspectives. But there were no windows to open.

My Role

Fifteen years ago when I began my student teaching, I asked one of the teachers with whom I would be working exactly what he taught. Always the good student, I wanted to prepare my lessons in advance. Pen in hand, ready to write down text and chapter, I waited. But there was nothing to record. My supervising teacher, peering at me above his glasses, replied, "I teach people."

Today, his words reverberate in my mind as though in an echo chamber. It is not that we do not teach texts and chapters, nor that we do not teach commas and organization. We teach all this, and more, to people who come from different backgrounds and from different cultures who are developing at very different rates. Certainly, some materials more effectively promote learning than others; so do some techniques and strategies. Materials, techniques, and strategies, though, do not work separately and apart from human interactions.

This book explores these interactions by telling stories. Except for their names, the characters in these stories are real. Events, too, are exactly as I remember them. Although I collected my data carefully, my intention was not to be scientific. To me, knowledge gained from teacher inquiry is the same as knowledge gained from literature. In my stories, I wanted to show the richness and texture of high school life in all its complexity.

I was not always a teacher. For many years, I wrote poetry. Not because I thought I was a poet, but because I wanted to understand my life. As a very young woman, I settled on an island at the tip of New Jersey and became the mother of three children. Sometimes on February days when the ocean appeared as gray as the sky and the houses across the street were boarded shut for the winter, my situation seemed, to me, incomprehensible. When my son napped and my two daughters played outside, I would write: poems about birds poised on telephone wires or flowers that bloomed from unremembered bulbs. Writing was the only way I knew to figure out my world. When I wrote I began to see beneath surfaces, to identify patterns. When I wrote, I began to understand.

Writing and discovering the truth became synonymous for me. An example of how my writing has been affected by my desire to get at the truth is the following excerpt from an essay I began about becoming a teacher:

> No one's ever asked me, "Why are you a teacher?" Not my parents, my children, my students, nor my closest friends. Maybe they thought it would be like asking me, "Why are you tall?" I suppose, like most of us, they've made up their own reasons anyway.
>
> I wish they had asked me, though. Answering them, I might have discovered why. Now, it's more complicated. For the first time, I'm questioning myself. Reflecting on my teaching, I want to tell my story. Yet, similar to telling my students' stories, because of the complexities, it's difficult to focus. Why I became a teacher is as hard to explain, has as many answers and is the result of as many interactions, as why my students have learned, or not learned, to become better writers.
>
> Surely, it's not surprising that I became a teacher. As far back as I can remember, I liked to work with kids. I wrote scripts, sold tickets, and staged backyard plays for the neighborhood toddlers, in which they starred, when I was seven. At eleven, I pushed my baby sister Paula's stroller from ten to twelve each morning while I taught her all the verses of "Davey Crockett." For my first job outside the neighborhood, I was Aunt Joycie, a counselor at the local day camp, Camp-by-the-Sea. The year before I started college, I worked for the city as a playground instructor—arts and crafts in the mornings and pick-up PIG on the basketball court in the afternoons. In high school, I was even elected president of the Future Teachers of America.

Rereading these three paragraphs, after I had finished writing them, I realized that they were not the complete truth. So, I dug down further:

> Although all these memories are true, they are not the truth. The truth is more complicated. Like many women who grew up middle-class in the fifties, I thought that teaching and nursing were the only respected jobs that were available to women outside the home. Teaching, rather than nursing, was presented to me as something I could always fall back on, a career that could be combined with a husband and children if I ever had to work,

or with children if my marriage failed or my husband died. Even now as I write this, I can hear the worried tone in my mother's voice. "Joyce, we never know what life has in store for us. You should always have something to fall back on. Someday you may have to work, and teaching is a good thing for a woman to do." Mother always said "thing" when she gave this lecture; she never said "career" or "profession."

Every once in awhile the girl-child in my head, the one who was lectured by her mother, feels confused. After all, if she had been able to do things right, if she hadn't messed up or made wrong turns in her life, she would never have had to teach in the first place. Her mother had taught her that teaching was respectable work, nothing to aspire towards, but something to fall back on. It's not surprising then that even though as far back as I can remember I have enjoyed working with kids, even though I was probably cut out to be a teacher in the first place, I am sometimes ambivalent about my job.

William Zinsser in his preface to *Writing to Learn* discusses the threefold nature of the writing process:

> I thought of how often as a writer I had made clear to myself some subject I had previously known nothing about by just putting one sentence after another — by reasoning my way in sequential steps to its meaning. I thought of how often the act of writing even the simplest document — a letter, for instance — had clarified my half-formed ideas. Writing and thinking and learning were the same process.

According to Zinsser, writing and thinking and learning the truth about why I had become a teacher were one and the same.

In a similar way, in order to tell stories about my teaching, I have had to be true to the person who I am — a woman who has lived for half a century, who gets angry, who loves, and who is fascinated by the strengths and foibles of herself and others. In order to learn from my own stories, I have had to slip off my professional mask and let you, my readers, see more than Mrs. Lott, the teacher. Too often in my windowless classroom or while moving through the crowded halls of South

Brunswick High School at the insistence of the bell, I have felt as though only a portion of me existed there. I have to be whole in order to tell stories, and I have to feel whole in order to teach.

Often, as a teacher, this has been difficult. Encouraging my students to discover their own topics, I trusted that form would follow content. Of course, this didn't always happen. Thinking of essays as exploratory in nature, I had not yet become aware of the processes through which we learn to shape and support our ideas.

Finding myself—as a writer and writing teacher—in the midst of a fairly traditional high school English department, I became deeply confused. Students were being taught that they should have a thesis before beginning to write and that they should develop their arguments logically in well-constructed paragraphs with proper transitions. Furthermore, they were encouraged not to use *I* and to support what they said with quotations that had been fully explained. Although most of this seemed to make good sense, I knew that I wrote differently. However, when I told my colleagues this or showed them essays that had been written in the first person or in which the thesis had not been stated in the opening paragraph, I often found myself in the midst of a dispute in which I was a minority of one. Having had little experience in such situations, I backed off, even though I knew that students were being denied the fun of writing: the act of discovery.

The task I set for myself was to reconnect students to their work—to show them that organization was not a final goal, that writing could be enjoyable and even personally important. I approached reconnecting them to their work by sharing my own writing with classes, encouraging them to choose their own topics, and stressing revision. Since I saw myself as a writer, I envisioned my students as writers. Also, I kept on learning—from workshops, from reading in the field, and from opportunities provided by my school district. I often learned from my mistakes, as in the stories of Jennifer and Liz. Most of all, though, I learned from my students, who are what all these stories are about.

Part One

Making Mistakes

Their story, yours, mine — it's what we all carry with us on this trip we take, and we owe it to each other to respect our stories and learn from them.

— William Carlos Williams to Robert Coles

Jennifer

Black Hats, Ribbons, and Being Herself

*S*ometimes I feel as though I should not be a teacher because I make too many mistakes. That is the feeling I had when I was teaching Jennifer. My intuition, which I could usually trust, became unreliable with her. What's more, after a year of attempts, I never felt I succeeded in clearly communicating with her. Jennifer's writing didn't seem to progress. Instead, after my comments, her revisions became less interesting or polished than her original drafts.

Jennifer's writing might have advanced more if I had used the portfolio system I now use with my students. Each marking period, Jennifer's portfolio would have been assessed, and she would also have had the opportunity to continue to work on individual pieces for her next portfolio. In this way, Jennifer would have been encouraged to get her papers "right." In addition, in each portfolio she would have written an essay of self-evaluation that took into account her work as a whole, instead of just evaluating individual papers. But, of course, hindsight is clearer. All I remember when I think of Jennifer are my mistakes.

When I first met her in September, Jennifer didn't stroll into senior Academic English chomping gum after the bell rang. Nor did she wear Grateful Dead t-shirts and torn jeans. Jennifer showed no stereotypical signs of rebellion or unwillingness to learn. She was freckle-faced, friendly, and full of enthusiasm for the year ahead. Jennifer sat next to her best friend Laura, amid a semicircle of people she had known most of her life, radiating confidence and promise. In a few months, she was to get the lead in the school play.

Jennifer's first paper, "Black Hats and Ribbons," was a sensitive portrait of how Meryl, a friend who had been killed in an automobile accident the summer before, had affected her life. Jennifer not only described her friend, but also herself, as can be seen by these opening paragraphs:

> I remember walking through a store running my fingers over a thick green cable knit sweater. Turning around, a black hat caught my eye. A thick black ribbon crowned it and came to a large bow in the front. Trying it on I wondered if I could get away with wearing it.
>
> "What will the people at school think of me wearing this?" I asked my sister Karen.
>
> "Jennifer, if Meryl taught you anything, wasn't it to be yourself and not care what other people think."
>
> Karen was right. Many times when I sit in my room staring at my hat, I try to rationalize why wearing it means so much to me. It's almost as though Meryl is there telling me to be proud of who I am.

Jennifer closed her essay this way:

> That hat has triggered so many memories, so many feelings. Now that I think of it, that black hat with the big black bow in the front, the hat that I was so reluctant to buy, almost represents a piece of Meryl. You know, I think I'll wear it tomorrow.

Jennifer's paper received a B + with this general comment: "Your paper only needs a little work. The tone is light enough so as not to make it sentimental and the hat provides the perfect framework. I hope you choose it for your revision. That should assure you an A for your double grade."

Mistake #1: Telling Jennifer that her revision "should assure" her an 'A', thus substantially promising her a grade in advance of a paper. My excuses: I liked Jennifer's paper and had confidence in her ability. Also, I had confidence in my own ability as a teacher. If Jennifer responded to my marginal comments and conferenced with me, she couldn't help but have a better paper—or so I thought.

Jennifer worked on her revision, adding details. In one instance, she described Meryl's "golden hair falling over her hummel-like face." "She looked like that," Jennifer told me during our conference, thrilled that she had thought of the comparison. Complimenting Jennifer on what she had done, I skimmed over her paper, circled a few technical errors and suggested that she team up with a friend, who wouldn't mind acting as a peer editor, before handing in her final copy.

At this point, Jennifer was, by my observation, a turned-on student. She continued to work, even after our conference, and a week later handed in her revision. There was a problem, though, that I had not anticipated. Jennifer had risked new ways of expressing herself and, in some places, had written over her head. There was no parallel structure in a few of the sentences she had combined, and there were tense problems in her paper where none had been before.

I was also over my head, and I knew of no way to reward Jennifer for the risks she had taken. I had not reflected sufficiently on the revision process to realize that the second draft of a paper, even after teacher comments, is not always "better" than the first. Nor had I come to the conclusion that only by studying a portfolio of work, preceded by an essay in which the writer has described her efforts, can I begin to see progress.

I wanted to be fair, fair to all my students, not easier on some than on others; I did not want to favor Jennifer. Therefore, I didn't give Jennifer the A I had so unwisely promised. Instead, I gave her the same B+ that she had received on her original paper with the comment, "Jen, don't let this grade get you down. Your description of Meryl is much fuller—it's just that in attempting to do so much (and I really admire the attempt!) you made errors in grammar and punctuation. Study my comments and consult your handbook. Keep working on this and send it to the school literary magazine. I would love to see it published."

I don't know if Jen kept working on "Black Hats and Ribbons" or sent it to the school literary magazine, although I suspect she did neither. What I do know, however, is that after I returned her paper she reacted differently to me, more negative, challenging my ideas in class and making all kinds of sarcastic facial expressions with her expressive actor's face. I wrote in her file near the end of November, "I feel as though not raising Jen's grade has bothered her a lot, because she conferenced with me and worked hard. Her behavior toward me has been different ever since — sort of an 'I can't please her anyway' or a 'she doesn't like me, so why should I try' kind of attitude."

Shortly after, I told Jen that I wanted to speak with her after class. When the other students left the room, I asked her if anything was wrong — was she angry with me? She shrugged, looking at me as though I came from another planet. "Come on, Jen. I'm not imagining things. I can see those faces you make while I'm talking," I said.

"That's the way I am," she replied. "Besides, I have a lot on my mind now with the play and all."

Thus far, by my own estimate, I had made three mistakes: (1) impulsively promising Jennifer an A on her revision, (2) not anticipating that revising sometimes creates other problems, and (3) not clearly communicating my dilemma to her. Beyond this, I wondered at the time if I had made a fourth mistake: making Jennifer's required revision her final grade on that particular paper.

What then, as teacher, should I have done when I knew I had made three mistakes and had not yet learned enough to know if I had made a fourth? The only answer I could come up with at the time was to behave the way I had when I failed geometry tests in high school — feel bad, talk to some people to try to get help, suffer the consequences, and hang in there.

Going along with all four of these behaviors, I waited for Jennifer's second marking period revision, an analysis of Goethe's *Faust*. When she handed her original paper to me, she said, "You're going to love this, Mrs. Lott." Jennifer's words sounded like a gesture of forgiveness. "Maybe it was worth hanging in," I thought.

Just as Jennifer was her own person, this was her own paper—no ordinary, run-of-the-mill analysis; instead, the paper took an original look at what Jen called Faust's inferiority complex. Jen began with an anecdote about an imaginary third grader named Fred, who was met by his mother when he got off the school bus and lied to her about his day over milk and cookies, all the time dreaming of the achievements of others.

Although Jen's paper was clever, she still had some technical errors that a better editing job could have picked up, and in some instances her language was unclear. Also, unlike her autobiographical essay, in this paper Jen's conclusion was weak. In my general comments to her, I wrote, "You're right. I love your paper! You are a most refreshing student to teach, but you must attempt to present a proofread paper without mechanical errors."

Jen understood and handed in her revision, carefully edited as required. There were no mechanical errors. But unlike the unrewarded risk that she had taken on her last paper, Jen did not actually revise. Instead, she stapled a revision idea for her conclusion to her title page, but did not make any structural changes. Jen had learned the lessons I had taught her first marking period: Don't stretch. Don't try anything new. Don't take risks when you write. Just fix up the surface of your paper. That's what English teachers want—they give out the grades, but they don't give out another chance.

As upset as I was about the message I had mistakenly given, I still assumed the odds were that I would eventually do something right. I planned to teach *A Streetcar Named Desire* next. Jennifer volunteered to play Blanche when we read it aloud in class. As I listened to her I could not help but fantasize that someday she would perform the play for a larger audience than Room C102. Jennifer *was* Blanche—her southern accent, her phoniness, her fragility covered with a veneer of charm. "I really like her," Jennifer told the class. "I love playing bitches, even though Blanche isn't really a bitch — she just acts that way."

Like all good actors, Jennifer got to know her character well, and when the time came to choose paper topics, she wanted to write about Blanche. She told me that she thought she would write her paper around the paper lantern motif, something that we had discussed in class. To Jennifer it was a complicated symbol: she saw Blanche as the light as well as the paper lantern that covered it. An in-class writing of Jennifer's revealed the germination of this idea:

> I think the light bulb is like the metaphor for Blanche. It's really subtle and one might think the metaphor is the paper lantern but I think that the lantern is kind of like the "mask" that Blanche wears. Blanche tries to hide herself behind flashy clothes and snotty airs because she doesn't want people to know about the real Blanche. When she says, "I can't stand a naked lightbulb, anymore than I can a rude remark or a vulgar action," I think she's saying she hates herself and sort of thinks of herself as something dirty and bad.

Jennifer attempted to work this idea into a paper. I was as excited as she. Jennifer's idea seemed lucid and fresh. The possibilities for a paper were excellent. When we met in the English office for a writing conference after Jennifer had begun work on her paper, she shoved her rough draft in front of me. Suggesting that she read it aloud, I listened. Her disorganized sentences, some original and others hackneyed, fell one on top of another into a marvelous mess. And the disorderliness was not just in what Jennifer had to say; it was also in the way she said it. In the two pages that Jennifer read aloud, she moved back and forth from personal to academic voice, in one paragraph using *I* and in the next *one*. Listening, I wondered how it could all be straightened out. I began by telling her that I had learned something from what she read, because I had never thought of Stella, whose name means star, in terms of light. If Stella was the light, as Jennifer said in her paper, what then did this have to do with Blanche covering up the light with a paper lantern? I really wanted to know.

As Jennifer explained her interpretation to me, I realized it was the first communication we had had all year as equals. I truly wanted to know what Jennifer meant by what she had written, and she clarified her ideas. When the period drew to a close, she said, "This is going to take all night. Can I show it to you again tomorrow?" Hearing that she was excited, that she couldn't wait to begin, I felt as though she was once again the enthusiastic student who had entered my class in September, the one who had written "Black Hats and Ribbons." Before I made my mistakes.

But there was still another issue — Jennifer's writing voice. I pointed out the dichotomy by reading aloud parts of her paper while she listened. Then I wrote "voice" with exclamation marks at the top of her draft, so that she wouldn't forget to think about it while she was revising. Treating her as a fellow writer, I told her that sometimes I have the same problem: I have discovered that when my voice is stilted and inconsistent, my ideas are often unclear. Just then the bell that ends the period rang. By the expression on her face and with her body language, Jennifer told me that she felt pretty helpless with this "voice" idea and needed to talk further with me about it in writing lab the next day.

That night I wrote in Jen's file, "I'm anxious to see how Jennifer organizes her paper. Obviously, the topic is personal. Jennifer, the actor, hides behind a lantern; both she and Blanche are not comfortable showing their vulnerability to the world. Certainly, I've suffered the brunt of Jen's defenses in the past months. Will she be able to analyze Blanche on paper? I'm curious to see what kind of start she gets."

I never did get to see the start of Jennifer's paper, because she never showed up for her second writing conference. When I saw her in class and asked why she hadn't kept her appointment, she blew me off with, "I don't need any help. Besides, I was busy sixth period." All I saw was Jennifer's final essay. The first four paragraphs follow exactly as she wrote them:

In "A Streetcar Named Desire" by Tennessee Wiliams I began to wonder if the character Blanche DuBois was really as awful as everyone thought. It later became apparent that how she appeared when she visited Stella was really how she was but not what she had become.

Blanche and Stella were brought up in the South and lived on a large plantation called Belle Reve. As girls, the two were very close and loved each other. A time did come, however, when Stella needed to leave to make a place for herself in the world. Blanche was left to fend for herself and to deal with the deaths in her family.

When Blanche was young she fell in love and married a young poet boy. She loved him dearly but she found out something that was very shocking to her. She walked in on her husband and another man during their homosexual encounter. At a banquet after her discovery, she called him a weakling while they were dancing. Her husband broke away from the dance, went outside and shot himself in the head. Blanche always blamed herself for his death.

In the town of Laurel Blanche was a school teacher. After the devestation from her dead family and husband, she began to look for affection, any affection, from many men even a 17 year old boy. In the Hotel Flamingo she brought her men and had many affairs. Towards the end of the play Blanche said, "I've always relied on the kindness of strangers," and during the time before her visit to Elysian Fields, she did.

The remainder of her paper consisted of the same carelessly written retelling of plot with a few insights here and there. "Why does Jennifer always make me feel like the world's worst teacher?" I asked in my journal. "None of the potential in the draft she read to me had been realized. I left our conference on a high, feeling good about our dialogue. What mistakes did I make this time?"

Mistake #?: Assuming that all seventeen year olds are capable of unraveling the yarn of conversation and then going home and tediously knitting it back into an original pattern. Jennifer had told me that it would take "all night" to get her paper right. She was a young girl with talent, insights, and little writing experience. My mistake had been to assume that she knew more than she did—that she was willing to work harder than she had.

Our freshman English teachers warn students against retelling plots, and our high school curriculum stresses organization. Why then did Jennifer, a senior, write as though she had never been exposed to this?

I require a self-evaluation to be handed in with every paper. In it, students record the amount of time they spent on that paper, the number of drafts they did, what they tried to improve or experiment with, questions they still have, and what they think the strengths and weaknesses of that paper were. In her self-evaluation, Jennifer wrote, "I tried to stay in the I voice, yet I didn't want to use the word/letter I." My interpretation of Jennifer's dilemma goes something like this: throughout elementary and middle school, Jennifer and her classmates had become experts in using "the word/letter I" because the personal narrative was the most common form of writing. It wasn't until Jennifer came to high school that she was taught to concentrate on more analytical writing and to support her ideas without writing *I think* and/or *I feel*. In order to teach this more effectively, Jennifer's high school teachers discouraged her from using *I*. Judging from her paper and from some of the papers of her classmates, Jennifer had the misconception that writing in first-person meant rambling on in a disorganized fashion. As a senior in a writing curriculum where she was encouraged to choose the form of her paper, Jennifer was confused.

I was confused as well. If I had used the portfolio system and Jennifer had evaluated her work as a whole, she and I both might have seen progress. After all, Jennifer never repeated the same mistake; instead, she made new ones. Jennifer did progress—one step forward and two steps backward the way most of us do—but she and I never got to see the whole picture. We only saw our mistakes.

Liz

The Moon Girl

My illusion is to become a famous five foot eight runway model with long silky-smooth tanned legs that never end, huge, luscious lips that could easily peal ripe grape skins, flowing blond hair with a lock of curls reaching down the curve of my back, and flawless skin as of that of a newborn baby's bottom. I would travel to exotic places, wear clothes people only dream of wearing, meet the most famous people in the world, have a beautiful, supportive husband, money that keeps us more than comfortable, and happiness that is everlasting, but unfortunately there is reality.

Reality is going to college, hoping, praying, and striving to make the cheerleading team, hoping to make the grades, parents breathing down my neck trying to make the right decisions for me, partying a little bit, then again busting my ass for the grades, then landing a good job.

Perceptive, honest, and adult, these two paragraphs sound as though they might have been lifted from the pages of a romantic novel. Instead, they were written by a seventeen year old. Bright and talented, Liz exhibited many traits of mature writers. She took risks in her writing, chose her topics with integrity, and accepted and learned from criticism. Even though her writing skills were not as well developed as they might have been, in many ways, Liz exemplified the ideal writing student. The only thing that detracted from this picture was her illusive desire for instant adulthood. It seemed as though Liz thought she could be an adult if she had access to adult things— "a beautiful, supportive husband, money that keeps us more than comfortable, and happiness that is everlasting. . . . " Obviously, Liz's idea of adulthood was a teenage fantasy. For her, becoming an adult involved finding shortcuts; it did not necessarily involve working hard. This philosophy affected her writing.

From the start, Liz had to let me know how mature she was. As one of the few students who chose Kate Chopin's novel *The Awakening* from the summer reading list, she wrote about the text with authority. Impressed that Liz could understand the yearnings of a nineteenth-century married woman as well as she did, I complimented her by saying, "Chopin's novel is a difficult book that wasn't appreciated in its own time. I remember when feminists discovered it in the sixties and gave it the publicity it deserved."

"I thought the woman in the novel lived before her time," Liz told me, "like myself. I think I'm too mature and want too many adult things. That's why I related to the book."

"What do you mean?" I asked her.

"Some guys think 'Oh, let's get to know her; she's pretty.' Yes, but what about my inside? On the inside, I have a lot to offer. It really pisses me off when guys do that."

I thought to myself that the problems nineteenth-century women experienced have continued in other forms in our own times.

In Liz's first paper, she described her grandfather, an immigrant from Czechoslovakia. "He was the person who influenced me," she said. "My grandpa was not only wise, he was down to earth. A real person, a real story." In her paper, though, Liz only told a little of her grandfather's "real story." Instead, she described her feelings toward him in clichéd terms that were mixed with eloquent and honest expression, as in the final paragraphs:

> My grandpa, had it hard, to put it plain and simple. I do not think I could have endured any one of the hardships he did. I can not comprehend how I thought I was so close to someone and yet their life was so different. Some times it makes me wonder and feel worthless, because I have had so few strives in my life, if any. Everything that I have has been handed to me on a silver platter, since I am an only child. I am not saying that I do not

appreciate what I get, I just wish that I could greatly understand and feel the agony of strife that he went through. I not only admire him, but all the other men, women, and children who came over for the chance of a lifetime, a new chance for freedom.

Although my grandfather has been gone for two years now, I will never forget the story he has strewn upon my mind. I just want to say one last thing and that is to thank you grandpa. In a few hours, with one story, you managed to change my whole outlook on life. I think if you were here at this moment you would be proud of me, as I was of you, to have been your grand-aughter. Your story has helped me develope some values and morals in my life and for that, your memory will always be tucked in my heart forever.

I filled the margins of Liz's paper with comments, many questioning misused words, several explaining how clichés, such as "your memory will always be tucked in my heart forever" can detract from real expression of feeling. My final comment: "Buried in all the words you've written is a wonderful story about your grandfather. I want to see him (as I did when he clutched the leatherbound chair) and hear him. Stick with your grandfather and his words. By implication, the reader will know how you feel. I promise."

Upset with her grade of C– and my comments, Liz nevertheless revised her paper. When she handed it to me a second time, she volunteered that she thought "it came out pretty well." I thought so, too. What follows are her revised concluding paragraphs:

"Life was hard and money was the key to many things," he would constantly say to me. After only two years of being here another ordeal came upon my grandpa, the U.S. draft. He was once again leaving, but this time he left another loved one behind with a hopeful promise of a safe return, his wife. (How much can a man handle I ask myself?) He continued his story with the telling of the bloodshed of the war. "I remember hearing the painful screams of men, crying out loud for their last gasps of air. I still sometimes can hear the constant buzzing of my gun in my ears, killing the enemy, which was someone who I did not even know, but hated with a passion. The only thing I learned from the war was how precious life can be, because in the blink of an eye it can be gone," he sadly stated.

After returning from the war, my grandfather started a family. He raised two sons, one of whom is my father. With luck, he landed a job at Triangle Cable and from there on his life prospered. Some of his earnings went into the stock market and he successfully tripled his money. "My dream came true. I have a family that I love and I worked damn hard to get it! I may be a no good foreigner that does not know too much, but I survived and made my dreams, hopes, and goals come true." So spoke my grandpa with such pride that his head stood straight up on his neck. A huge smile broadened his face, and he looked at me while he winked with his right eye and saluted me with his left.

Weeks later, when Liz came to discuss her next paper, Heather, a classmate, was already standing at my desk. "That can't be a cliché, Mrs. Lott," Heather was arguing while she pointed to a line of poetry. "I thought of it myself."

Taking over my role, Liz explained to Heather, "You might think you've thought of it yourself, but that's probably because you've heard it a lot." "I understand about clichés now," Liz continued. And then she asked me with confidence, "May I *imply* in this next paper, Mrs. Lott?"

Although Liz seemed to learn new ideas, her efforts were sporadic. Whether she worked or not often depended on what was happening with her boyfriend or what was going on at home. Half adult and half child, Liz sometimes presented a confusing picture.

Dear Mrs. Lott,

I just wanted to inform you that I would not be handing in my paper today, but Monday. I honestly can say that I forgot about it until Monday and I started it on Tuesday, but that just wasn't enough time. I don't want to hand in anything that I don't feel comfortable with because I know I'll get a bad grade. In actuality, we are not supposed to be doing the paper for the grade, but for what we put into it. I don't want you to think that

I'm blowing off this assignment. I just want to give you my best work. Like when I handed in that Ibsen paper I did horrible, because I didn't go with it. I didn't like what I wrote, so this time I wanted to be sure. I just wanted to let you know. Thanks for taking the time to read this.

Love,
Liz

This note is an example of Liz at her most confusing. Sometimes I was not sure what she was actually saying: Was she careless about the paper or did she care about it? How could I reply? Never quite sure how to reply to late papers, I followed the procedure we had discussed in English department meetings, finally giving Liz a D (a half grade down for each day it was delayed). Accepting the grade graciously, she told me, "I thought my introduction was good, but I got bored toward the end."

Liz did not get bored with our next activity, though. In the process of being trained by my district in cooperative learning techniques, I structured an exercise in which groups of three to five students analyzed two of Wordsworth's sonnets and then wrote a paper together comparing and contrasting the sonnets. Different from traditional competitive learning, cooperative learning emphasizes heterogeneous groups in which there is shared responsibility. Before the class began working, I gave them an enthusiastic pep talk. "Working well in groups is a quality that employers are looking for," I told them. "Big companies are giving training programs in cooperative learning. In the workplace, just as in other adult situations, there is always shared responsibility."

Since that particular assignment I have gained more experience with cooperative learning techniques and now realize the complication of a group paper that requires work outside of class; in fact, I am surprised that they were even able to complete the task. But Liz never worked harder. Her goal was clear—it was an adult task, not just schoolwork. In fact, her group was so enthusiastic that they asked if they could do something different: a simulation of a television broadcast. Not only did Liz use her talent as an artist to create visual materials, but she searched out biographical data on Wordsworth as well. Yearning for any semblance of adulthood, Liz wrote on her self-evaluation, "I really tried to understand everybody. I liked working in the group, because it showed me that when I get older I will be a very personable person who will be able to work in a group situation well."

Although Liz remained "a very personable person," her standard of work fluctuated during the second half of senior year even more than it had during the first semester. No longer focusing on the niceties of implication, avoiding clichés, or becoming a supportive member of a cooperating group, Liz focused almost entirely on Avinash, a student who sat next to her in English class. He, too, was bright and personable. But unlike Liz, Avinash was failing because of incomplete work. During the second semester of her senior year, Liz's role in English class changed from my student to Avinash's savior. Liz might have felt like an adult, but her English skills did not improve.

"Why don't you ask Jane or Stephanie to edit your paper?" "Why don't you use a dictionary?" "Why don't you get a spellcheck?" "Why don't you review where the punctuation goes in quotations?" I reread my comments up and down the margins of her second semester papers. Little did I know at the time I was wasting my energy! By April, I was at my wit's end.

In order to expose the class to a variety of books (they were reading little outside of class), I brought in several copies of five different novels, inviting them to select the one they most wanted to read. Discussing each book with them, I mentioned that Carolyn Chute's novel, *The Beanes of Egypt, Maine*, might be offensive to some because of the harsh realities of life it depicted. Liz, of course, chose it immediately.

Two weeks later, Liz discussed in an in-class essay how *The Beanes of Egypt, Maine* had helped her to better understand life, writing perceptively and with strong feeling about how love was expressed in the novel.

17

In conclusion I feel that when you have no love in your family, you go out searching for it. The funny part is that you always end up with someone you're not supposed to be with. In Earlene's . . . case the Beane family, in my case Avinash. I've been hurt and I wasn't looking for anyone, but we just got together, and we've been that way ever since. Once you find that solid love you never want to let go, because I don't think I could ever be happier. In my father's eyes it's wrong, just like Earlene, but how can you say any love is wrong. It's not. In a sense, I feel what Earlene feels. I can relate to her. I'm glad she stayed with the Beane family. She loved them and they loved her. Even though my Dad doesn't agree (doesn't know) I can't let him ruin my happiness. It's not right, nor fair. I know he'd never stop loving me, I just have to make him understand and let go, like Earlene did. I have to admit, she's one brave kid.

After reading this, I decided to talk to Liz after school about Avinash. My rationales for doing so were that I cared about Liz and that her relationship with Avinash seemed to be affecting the quality of her work. In addition, I wanted to get things out into the open — to make Liz's life a part of school — rather than to have it stand in the way. After all, pretending to ignore what was really causing Liz problems in English class had proved ineffective.

"I hope you're not sacrificing yourself for a man," I began bluntly. "I've seen too many women do that. It's foolish."

"Oh, I'm not, Mrs. Lott. Avinash wouldn't let me. He's one of the greatest human beings I've ever known."

"I like him, too, Liz. But your work's going downhill, and he seems to be all you can think of or write about."

"No, it's not that," Liz informed me. "It's my troubles at home." She then proceeded to tell me how her parents didn't know or didn't want to know that she was seeing Avinash, and how prejudiced her father was against guys who weren't "all-American types." "Especially brown-skinned men like Avinash," Liz concluded.

Acknowledging to Liz that what she was going through was real, I told her about my own marriage against my parents' wishes to a man who belonged to a different religion, the problems we have encountered, and how right that relationship has ultimately been for me. I also told her that college would be coming up before she knew it and that she would have to prepare herself if she wanted to succeed.

"Thanks, Mrs. Lott, for letting me talk about my true feelings," she said when we finished our conversation. "I hope one day Avinash and I can be as happily married as you and your husband are!"

Laughing to myself about the romantic nature of teenagers, I tried to imagine what illusions Liz had about my marriage. But whatever the connection to our conversation (if there was one) her next paper, an essay about Woody Allen's film *Annie Hall*, was not only handed in on time, it was also pretty good. Even though she did refer to Avinash and continued to choose an adult topic—she titled her paper: "Allen—That Little Sex Devil!"—her argument was sophisticated and her paper written with style. For the first time, Liz signed her full name on the title page—Elizabeth. Below are her opening paragraphs.

I am sitting cross-legged on the couch watching this eccentric Woody Allen movie with Avinash. It is hard to pay attention when you don't get any vibes from the main character, Alvie Singer, played by Allen, but when you get vibes from your partner who is watching the movie next to you. I try to focus on Allen, who is talking to his girlfriend, Diane Keaton, who plays Annie Hall. They are lying in her bed finishing from an intimit session of sexual intercourse. Annie mentions Alvie's first wife, Allison, "Alvie, you were very hot for Allison . . . ," Annie says, with this determined look of truth on her face. First of all, I am wondering who the hell is Allison? I thought this movie was about Annie Hall. All of a sudden, Blamo! Right after Annie makes her statement, I see Alvie talking to this red-haired, jewish girl with an annoying, nasily voice. She is slightly attractive. Alvie appears nervous and very unsettled like a nieve jewish boy waiting for his first train ride to manhood. He runs out on stage for his comedy routine, leaving Allison with a big smile on her face and says, "I've been trying to do to this girl what Eisenhowers been doing to this country." This sexual connotation, actually to put it bluntly "fucking," leads us to Allison and Alvie in bed fooling around.

After I watch these transitions, I finally figure out that Allen is being clever—telling us about his relationships through how his mind works, not through sequencing. This invention keeps my mind working, too. I want to get the "nitty-gritty" on Allen. Curious about his past relationships, about his non-stopping sexual drives and urges, I want to compare his present relationship with Annie to his past ones. In the movie "Annie Hall," director and star, Woody Allen, achieves his transitions by using stimuli from his present relationship with Diane Keaton (Annie Hall) to trigger past relationships and experiences.

In her self-evaluation, Liz wrote that she spent about five to six hours on the paper and switched topics three times. In reply to the question, "What did I try to improve or experiment with on this paper?" Liz answered, "I tried to put some Jewish humor in it." What interested me especially, though, was her journal entry on May 7.

I was upset when the class decided to watch "Annie Hall." I couldn't stand Woody Allen in the past, but I didn't think the movie was half bad. I'm so glad Mrs. Lott liked the paper, because I felt comfortable with it. I tried to add humer to my paper as Allen did to his movie. I think I also enjoyed it because it was a different pace for me. Usually my papers are serious, but this time I was able to let loose and just write about funny crazy things. I also learned that it is better to keep an open mind about something and this way when you decide your feelings about it, you know they're really true instead of a preconceived notion. Thanks to Mrs. Lott for her open mind. It rubbed off on me!

Apparently, Liz took my interest in her relationship with Avinash as an open-minded gesture. Although I did not expect our conversation to have an effect on Liz's writing, it did.

In spite of a slightly discernible improvement in her prose style, Liz did not achieve the growth in her writing I had anticipated. To Liz, studying English just didn't matter as much as becoming an adult and living in the "real world." Looking for a shortcut to adulthood, Liz wanted to get there fast. In this journal entry, Liz answered the question "How do you escape from yourself?"

> Getting away from my "self" . . . Hmm! Well now, I think the best way I accomplish this is driving, actually speeding. Especially, in the summer time. I open the windows and the sun roof and feel the cool wind whip my hair all over my face. The speed for me is like a time warp. I'm going through a zone where I can escape my "self" and be no one, just flesh. It's like in the movie "Flash Gordon" when they erased Hans Zarcoft's memory. The speed makes my life's actions run over and out of my mind. It's me alone out there with no one screaming to do better, or to not have so much free time, or about school. I like it. In a sense, I feel as though my body is with this world, but I am not. My mind is clear and empty. The speed cures all my woes and worries. The car is my guide and it takes me wherever I want to go. I always end up somewhere, usually in a park or at the beach, somewhere where the environment will have a positive effect on me. I guess speed and the machine are the cure and maybe my compass also.

I am still trying to answer the question our interaction posed: could I have taught Liz more effectively? As I look over her papers, it is clear to me that throughout the year her writing did not improve significantly, even though she had flashes of brilliance. Liz's work remained inconsistent; some of her finished papers still read like journal entries. I didn't help her to improve her writing, even though I commented on her papers profusely, to transmit my knowledge to the best of my ability. There were no problems interacting, either. Unlike my relationship with Jennifer, Liz and I seemed to get along fine. In a note to me at the end of the year, Liz wrote:

> I just wanted to tell you I've learned much in your class this year, and I am grateful. I honestly don't think most of my learning, though, had to do with English, but with things more on a personal level. Thank you for all your help with Avinash and that situation. Also, thank you for keeping on him to do his work!

And the final line read, "I want you to know you honestly helped me a great deal, because you let me grow and experience on an adult level."

Although Liz is unique in some ways, year after year male and female students like her sit in my classroom. Bright and perceptive, they are not nearly as interested in schoolwork as they are in growing up. Either in love, yearning for love, or depressed about an unhappy relationship, they don't see the importance of academic endeavors. Nor do they allow themselves the time or energy to focus on what I want to teach them. They are only interested in learning if the subject matter is connected to their immediate obsessions. Once in awhile, I make progress with them; most of the time, I don't.

Postscript

I originally ended Liz's story thus. But, when Peter Stillman, my editor at Boynton/Cook, returned my manuscript, he attached a post-it to the final paragraph: "I'd like to know Liz better as student, person. Can't get a very good fix on her or how you could possibly otherwise have reached her. I think the piece doesn't conclude the way either of us wishes. Shall we discuss?"

Damn him, I thought. He's got to realize I've agonized for months about how to conclude Liz's story. He must see that my own reflections have only led me around in circles. "Shall we discuss?" Wouldn't it be better to discuss Liz with someone who knew her?

I thought of Paul Clark, Liz's junior English teacher. Paul and I had talked about Liz two years before when I was teaching her. Paul had called her "bright," I remembered. And he doesn't label students "bright" often.

I reminded Paul of this. "Liz was bright all right. She had been bright all along. But what was wrong is what's wrong with so many students in our district. She never had to measure herself against objective standards. She had a provinciality about her that had been imposed by a school system that wouldn't open things up."

"Liz had no sense of herself, as with most juniors," Paul continued. "She would slip and slide back and forth into the same level of achievement. Liz's big transition was from tenth to eleventh grade, when for the first time she was hit with an objective model. I said she was bright because she was alert. She asked questions; she wanted to experience new things, even though she didn't always have the tools to accomplish what she wanted to learn. Her world was beginning to broaden."

And then Paul said something that I knew was the truth. "Liz was on the cusp of understanding. She had outgrown her perceptions of herself."

"She remained on the cusp, didn't she?"

"Yes," Paul answered. "If she had become a better student, she would have lost her community, her friends."

So that was why there were so many female and male Lizs in our district. Their world hadn't been broadened. And when they began to see how much they could learn, they became frightened. For if they acknowledged their intelligence they would become other than who they had been. They would no longer be a member of their community.

"On the cusp." Paul's phrase reverberated in my mind until in true English-teacher fashion I found myself standing in front of an opened dictionary. "Cusp: in astronomy, either horn of a crescent moon." Liz, the moon girl. The new-moon girl, balancing her position from tip to tip.

And then I began to think of the dichotomy of Liz: Liz, the adult; Liz, the child. I went back and read the two paragraphs I had chosen so many months ago to open Liz's story. "Dichotomy: in astronomy, that phase of the moon or of a planet in which only half of its apparently flat surface seems to be illuminated."

Liz, the moon girl. Why hadn't I been able to see this earlier? Was it because I, too, had been a moon girl for so many years?

Reflections

Sometimes I wish my talents lay elsewhere. I would like to build cabinets, for example, to smooth and finish wood that I have selected, and leave no rough edges. Picture a cabinetmaker standing back and admiring her work from every angle: cabinets shaped to fit the contour, measured, planed, and finely joined. Instead of making cabinets, though, I have taught over a thousand students in the course of ten years. And for some like Jennifer, I have never been able to mold the design or the outcome.

Unlike cabinetmakers, teachers rarely get to admire their finished work. Take Allison, for instance. Last year she stopped by school with her little daughter, as red-headed as Allison. "I'll never forget what you taught me," Allison said.

"Wait a minute, Allison," I rejoined, "you were in no state to be taught anything. All I did was sit with you on the steps of the alternative school's trailer, encouraging you to get that terrible temper of yours out on paper before you were kicked out of school."

"But you taught me so much," she insisted. "I still like to write. I'm married; I have a job, and a daughter with a temper." We both laughed.

Daniel Gottlieb, a clinical psychologist whose program "Family Matters" is on National Public Radio, would understand Allison's story. In his book *Family Matters* (1991), he writes on the final page that "healing in therapy is about 60 percent *who you are* and 40 percent *what you do*." Gottlieb goes on to say that "all people in the helping professions are somewhere on the continuum of healer." Although this statement is mystical, my experience as a teacher confirms it.

But understanding *who you are* takes a lifetime. There were a few strategies I might have employed, things I could have *done*, that would have helped my interactions with Jennifer and Liz. First of all, I should not have emphasized grading as much as I did even though, in a school system, grades are required. I realize now that grades might have inhibited both Jennifer's and Liz's learning. Peter Elbow (1986) has written about using grading to enhance learning. I am beginning to agree with his premise that grading everything a student writes is unnecessary. Students need to write; and, realistically, most teachers don't have the time to comment responsibly on everything a student composes. This approach might make writing more satisfying and less of a chore for teachers as well as students.

In addition to becoming more comfortable with the idea of not grading every paper, I have been searching for an approach to assessment that will allow for greater student involvement as well as a way to record student progress. At this point, I am dedicated to using portfolios (see "Using Portfolios," Part Five).

Varying reading assignments, showing films, and using diverse learning strategies was something I *did* that was beneficial. Students do not have uniform interests nor do they learn in the same way. Liz progressed after seeing *Annie Hall*; Jennifer, after performing the part of Blanche, appreciated *A Streetcar Named Desire*. For Liz, cooperative learning was effective; for Jennifer, individual work was more helpful.

Nevertheless, one way or another, I felt as though I should have been able to teach Jennifer and Liz more. In fact, of the students whom I studied over the course of the year, I felt that only a few of them learned what I would have liked. And my sampling did not include students like Kim or Laura. Much to everyone's surprise, Kim gave birth to a baby girl in February, left school, and was tutored at home. It was not until then that I realized why Kim had been so distant and uninterested in class. Laura found out in December that her recurrent stomach pains were caused by cancer. After her operation, she accomplished as much as she could. Although it would be foolish to pretend that my sampling was a scientific one, these observations at least help to explain why I — and other teachers — often feel frustrated. Results are not guaranteed.

I was raised on the aphorisms, "If you don't succeed at first, try, try again" and "the boys who have tried the most, make the world's best men." Practicing jump rope in the garage, where no one could see me miss, I got to be one of the best jumpers on the block. Later, memorizing theorems I would forget as soon as I turned in my test, I earned A's in geometry. I never questioned the fact that I could not be a man. Nor did I ever try to define "best." My professors at graduate school, the superintendent who interviewed me for my job, my principal, and both department supervisors who evaluated me never shared a terrible truth: on a regular basis, teachers have to cope with a sense of failure.

Part Two

Learning About Bias

We are in the middle of an extraordinary social experiment: the attempt to provide education for all members of a vast pluralistic democracy. . . . At heart, we'll need a guiding set of principles that do not encourage us to retreat from, but move us closer to, an understanding of the rich mix of speech and ritual and story that is America.

— Mike Rose, *Lives on the Boundary*

Rahul

Learning to Trust Himself

*R*ahul was a tall, handsome Indian student who did not have a friend in the class. Whenever the class paired up to edit their papers, Rahul was the one without a partner, not because he was not a good writer but because no one liked him. I didn't like him much either, but I would never have admitted this to myself if Rahul were not one of the students whose progress I was following particularly closely. There was something sneaky about Rahul. It was as though he had figured out a way to be in the classroom and disappear at the same time, sitting quietly in a chair that seemed to be just outside my line of vision, even when we all formed a circle. Some days he might literally absent himself, usually when a paper was due or when he was to return his partner's editing. Always, the following day, Rahul would arrive silently with the required paper and an excused absence note signed by his mother.

The only times when Rahul spoke directly to me, or to anyone in English class as far as I could observe, was after I returned papers. Then he would come up to my desk or into the English office and argue about his grade. "Why is this a B–?" he would ask.

"Have you read over my comments?" I would answer, having put as many comments on his paper as on any of his classmates'. Rahul's writing was wordy and repetitious. In each instance, I had remarked on this. Nevertheless, Rahul challenged his grade as though I had explained nothing. I wanted to shout at him in frustration, "Why can't you care about your writing as much as your grades? Why don't you want to please yourself instead of your parents?" But I didn't. Instead, I behaved like the fair, open-minded person I thought I was. "You'll have the opportunity to revise this," I told him. "Study my comments and keep working. When you hand in your revision at the end of the marking period, it can be another grade."

Early in the year, Rahul caught on that deletion is probably the easiest form of revision, especially when your teacher does the work. I would comment each time that Rahul was repetitious and verbose. Meticulously, he would check off my comments, one by one, handing in a clean revision. Unfortunately, though, Rahul learned nothing. His next paper would include fifteen typed pages of wordiness, repetition, and plot rehash. When I tried to read it, looking for Rahul's focus, I felt as though I were rooting through the trash looking for a lost spoon that had already been put in the dishwasher. Here is Rahul's introductory paragraph:

In the film "The Graduate," by Mike Nichols and Lawrence Turman, Benjamin Braddock, played by Dustin Hoffman, changed drastically as the film progressed. He changed from a person bottled away from his environment (not knowing what he wanted in life), to a person who sees what he wants and goes after it. Benjamin was a graduate fresh out of college, as the film begins. He was entering the real world, and he didn't know what to expect. He was a very confused young man, who was afraid of what his future held. In essence, he was bottled up in his own world just trying to blend into the pressure filled world around him. In school, he had never learned how to deal with family peer pressure. Right out of college, Benjamin had to deal with the pressures rendered on him by his parents and a family friend, Mrs. Robinson. These pressures caused him to become even more bottled away from the world than he already was. The pressures caused him to lose sight of his own needs and wants. As the film progressed however, Benjamin metamorphosized into a mature person, who had a grip on what he wanted in life.

Refusing to do Rahul's work for him, I scheduled a writing conference in the English office. "How will I let go of my biases against him?" I asked in my journal the night before. "This isn't like me. What's causing the aversion I feel?"

I began the conference by asking Rahul where he was applying to college and what he wanted to study. He smiled when he answered, his dark eyes sparkling. Rahul wanted to be a doctor. He was applying pre-med because he really liked science. I began to think, "It's my fault. This kid isn't so bad after all."

"I get As in science," he told me. "English causes me trouble."

"Why?" I asked.

"I was really good in it until ninth grade," he said. "We didn't have to analyze; we could just write—as much as we wanted."

I thought about Rahul with his extensive plot summaries, his pages and pages of details, hoping to achieve the perfect paper. Maybe that was what he was still doing.

But this was twelfth grade; he had been in high school for more than three years. I wasn't satisfied. "How can anyone who excells in science write papers the way you do? Doctors have to zero in on diseases. You're going to have to learn to do this with language."

Clearly, this wasn't the right approach, because immediately Rahul began to argue about his grade. I became more concrete. "Let's look at your introduction," I said. "Why did you think it was necessary to repeat three times that Benjamin was bottled up or bottled away?"

"You know, that was a trashy movie," Rahul retorted. "All that music and all that stuff."

"Huh?!" I thought. "What in the world is he talking about?"

Rahul continued. "Ben didn't break loose after his affair with Mrs. Robinson like everyone in class said. He didn't break loose until he lied to his mother that time when he was shaving. He knew he was wrong after that. You don't lie to your mother."

"Oh," I answered, still confused. "So that was the turning point. Where did you write that in your paper?" Rahul showed me. Among hundreds and hundreds of words, buried somewhere within all his plot summaries and details, he had discussed Ben's talk with his mother.

My problem as a reader had been that I had never seen what Rahul had written. At no point, while reading his paper, had I been on Rahul's wave length. I loved the movie— "all that music and all that stuff"— and so had most of my students. To put it simply, Rahul and I had not seen the same film. No Western viewer, used to graduates rebelling against their parents and lying to their mothers about where they had spent the night, would have seen Ben's short conversation with his mother as a pivotal point in the film. Rahul taught me that in his culture, mothers are given more respect than in ours. They have a greater influence on college graduates. Furthermore, because of his cultural values, Rahul found Ben Braddock's behavior with Mrs. Robinson too reprehensible to even consider important.

Rahul's problem was that he had been unable to assert this. In order to please the teacher who, he knew, did not understand him, in order to get the grade he needed to get into college, he included—word after word, repetition after repetition—"everything." He wasn't confident enough to emphasize his own view of the film's turning point.

Just as I was beginning to realize that our cultures were making us antagonists, Rahul began to argue about his grade once again. "I don't have time now. I have to get to class," I told him, "but let me know if you'd like another conference."

Rahul's grade on his revision did improve, but not until I had this dialogue with myself in my journal:

> This is one of those situations when I'm not sure I can be fair. I just don't like Rahul's writing style.
> *Okay, Joyce, be methodical—like Rahul. Did Rahul get rid of his wordiness?*
> Yes, pretty much.
> *Did he delete some passages that didn't focus on his thesis?*
> A few. He went from fifteen to thirteen pages!
> *Did he make it easier for the reader to follow his point?*

Yes, I guess so. He repeated it and proved it enough, but I wish he'd left out some of those pages of recorded dialogue and that business about Mrs. Robinson being the opposite of Ben's *real* needs and desires.

Do you think that you couldn't go along with that because you don't see things the way he does culturally?

Possibly, but I'm trying.

Okay, now. How are you going to grade him? What are you going to say?

You're really boring and overly verbose.

No, Joyce, you know you can't say that. His mother will call and you'll have a hell of a time explaining.

Okay, I'll give him a B, are you satisfied? I'll tell him that he corrected some of his wordiness (that's true) and now, even though there were some unnecessary examples that took away from his focus, it was easier to see his point. And do you know what's going to happen? Rahul is going to come to me and argue about why he didn't get an A.

But before Rahul had a chance to confront me, I began to wonder about other aspects of his behavior. Why is Rahul's speech so measured? He only speaks in class if I call on him. And why is his writing so repetitive? What could the relationship be between his speech and his writing? If Rahul could hear his own voice more often, would his writing be less wordy?

Journal writing proved to be a way to see these issues more clearly. Rahul, along with the rest of his class, was required to keep a journal over the three weeks that we studied Herman Hesse's *Siddhartha*, a book based on an ancient Buddhist journey toward enlightenment. At the beginning of Hesse's tale, Siddhartha, a young Hindu, left his family in order to escape from Self with a band of wandering ascetics. Continuing his search, Sid—as my students called him—persisted in trying to escape in more worldly ways until, as an old man, he accepted life in its totality.

It was in his journal that Rahul began to talk. Unlike his more formal papers, Rahul's journal writing was neither ponderous nor repetitive. It was clear and, at times, depressingly

33

honest. At the beginning of Hesse's novel, Siddhartha was wearied by the constant cycle of life. Here is the way Rahul responded:

> At this point, my life is a depressing, nerve-wracking cycle: birth, childhood, school, college, work, old age, and death. I am going to school to get an education and then a good job. My daily life consists of going to school, eating, and sleeping. My day to day life doesn't seem to change from month to month until summer vacation. Of course, after summer vacation, it's back to school. Sometimes I ask myself if it is really worth it to go through everyday life just so you can die at the end of the road. When I think about it, all the grades and education and money will not help me when I am on my death bed.
>
> Life is a cycle, a cycle beginning with birth and ending with death. Right now my cycle consists of going to school every day and every year. Hopefully, something different will happen in my life soon. A change of pace would be nice. Right now, I am trapped in my forever revolving cycle of a life.

Finally, while studying *Siddhartha*, Rahul had an opportunity to discuss his Hindu background. When the class questioned him, though, he was reticent. "My parents have been here a long time," he remonstrated. "It's my grandparents, back in India, who believe in all that stuff." Nevertheless, in the following passage from his paper "Listening: The Forgotten Art of Learning, in Relation to Siddhartha," written after I had returned his journal, Rahul asserted his own cultural experience.

> I have had many experiences in which I have learned by listening. One in particular stands out. It occurred a few summers ago when I visited my grandfather in India. Our days were spent working on the family farm and our nights were spent on the dark porch in front of the family house. My grandfather and I would spend our evenings making small talk about the farm and listening to a certain bird, who made its home in a tree in front of the house. Everyday the bird would make chirping noises as it tended to its young. I would listen to it, because I had nothing better to do. Then one day, I realized that the bird was teaching

its young to fly, as an ill prepared young one fell to its death from the tree. The bird continued to show its offspring how to fly, chirping as it ushered the next baby to try.

I realized a similarity between the bird teaching its young to fly and my grandfather teaching me the farmers' way of life. This may seem imagined, but the reality of the situation I was in was suddenly clear to me. I was the little one being taught by the elder. The many days that I spent listening to the bird made me realize what my purpose was in being in my grandfather's company. I had learned from listening. I hadn't learned Nirvana as Siddhartha had, but I had learned more about family relations and the process of the young learning from the old.

Here it was — clear, direct, honest — no pretense. Rahul trusted what he had to say; it was part of his own experience. He did not need to say it again and again. In my judgment, Rahul had taken a big step toward learning to write.

But Rahul was not just my student, he was also my teacher, teaching me about myself, about my profession, and also about language. The first thing he taught me was that I was not as open minded and tolerant as I would like to have been. He showed me that I enjoyed students who trusted me and wanted to learn. He demonstrated that I liked being with students who had ideas and values that were compatible with mine. Because Rahul tried to protect himself by hiding from me and his classmates, I had labeled him sneaky. Because he was more concerned about his grades than about the content of his work, I labeled him shallow. Rahul taught me about my own biases. He also taught me about myself as a writing teacher. Studying Rahul's work, I clearly realized that I prefer some writing styles over others. In the beginning, no matter how hard Rahul worked, I just didn't like his prose.

More than instructing me about the teaching of writing, however, Rahul taught me about teaching. He taught me that the way we express ourselves does not exist within a vacuum, that what we have to say and the way that we say it is connected to our cultural identity, personal identity, and sense of worth within the smaller culture of the classroom. Since teaching Rahul, I have learned that repetition is stylistically part of Indian rhetoric. Since the new world literature program, established after Rahul's graduation, studying other cultures should make it easier for future Rahuls to assert their own ideas.

In a curriculum that emphasizes a multiplicity of cultural values, students ought to feel encouraged to express a diversity of viewpoints. Not needing to hide what they really think, they should not feel compelled to obscure their ideas. Instead, students should be more comfortable expressing their thoughts to classmates and teachers whose mindsets are different than their own.

If I had been asked before I wrote about Rahul if I were biased against any of my students, I probably would have laughed and replied, "Maybe I like some better than others. That is only natural, but I would not want them to be alike. Differences make teaching fun." As a teacher/researcher documenting my interactions with Rahul, I discovered biases that I had managed to hide, even from myself. Although he doesn't know it, Rahul taught me valuable lessons in the course of my study.

Joseph

A Foreigner From the Surface

In November of his senior year, Joseph turned in this paper, telling of his Sundays in Hong Kong. His writing looked like this:

> I used to go to my father's hospital to study every Sunday. I woke up early in the morning, ate my breakfast, got on the bus, and took the ferry across the harbour to his hospital. That was the funnest part of each long Sunday. After I greeted the nurses and doctors, I had to walk up a five stories building to go to his room. I could've take the elavator, but my father said walking up stairs is a good excited, and I agreed with him. The desk in his room that I used face at the airport less than a mile away. Every three minutes, a plane would fly above my head and landed gracefully. Behind me, there was a TV that was never turned on when my books were opened. While I was studying, he would sit on the bed and read his medical books because there was only one chair in the room. Before we had our dinner in his room, he would give tests of what I had study for that afternoon. If the test results were unsatisfactory, the food would just sit there until I got a B or above. We would eat and talked until 8 o'clock because I had to catch the 8:30 bus to get to the ferry port to across the harbour. He would walk to the bus stop with me. He wouldn't leave until the bus I was in could no longer been seen from his eyes.
>
> I thought of these Sundays a lot when I am studying along in the United States. No airplane is landing before me, nobody is giving me anymore tests before dinners, and no father can again easily appear before me.

Joseph had been in the United States with his mother and sister for two years when he wrote these words. In this new family arrangement, Joseph was the one who was supposed to achieve, the one who was destined to carry on the family name. Joseph's father, a doctor, remained in Hong Kong. Fearful that he would be unable to practice medicine in the United States and make the money that he thought his family needed, he chose to support them from across the sea. Already, he had bought his son a fine computer on which Joseph did his homework. At home, Joseph kept his computer locked in his room; in school, he spent his spare time, including lunch, assisting Lester Ray, the high school technology supervisor. There was no thought in Joseph's mind but that he would do everything in his power and work as hard as he could to be a successful son.

Joseph's training and drive for success made teaching him a pleasure; conversely, these same factors created problems, problems I was not fully aware of until I began telling his story. How do public schools provide for students who arrive during their junior or senior year and who have not had the same training as their peers? In Joseph's case, he spoke English well enough not to be placed in our English-as-a-second-language program—a course reserved for those who did not know the language—but not well enough to be comfortable in the classroom. In addition, he had little training in writing expository essays, while his classmates had been trained in various expository forms for over three years. The curriculum I was teaching was probably inappropriate for Joseph, but he had no other choice.

Joseph's biggest problem, though, was his isolation. He wanted to fit in, but not as a recent immigrant or as an Asian-American. He wanted to be accepted as an American high school student. And, even more than total acceptance, Joseph wished for a friend.

However, I knew nothing about Joseph when he was placed in my class in September. All I knew was what I could observe: Joseph was quiet and thin. It was not until I read his first paper that I realized his English skills were deficient. On Joseph's first essay, an autobiographical narrative about the friend he had been forced to leave in California, I wrote numerous comments and ended by saying, "I can't give you the grade you deserve because of the problems I have listed. You do have many strengths in the paper already, though— your dialogue is good and so are your similes and metaphors." Because he had chosen an academic English class, I knew that Joseph wanted to go to college. I also knew that he would have a hard time staying there because of his writing. Joseph's first narrative paper during his senior year began like this:

> "Stop! Stop!" Danny was yelling and braceing himself with his arms at the front door, as his father was punching him like a boxer boxing in a ring. Blood was splashing from his noise when his father gave him a right hook punch. The next thing he remembered was that he was lying on a white bed with patients around him. Tears were dripping from our eyes as he was telling me this story that happened one year ago before I went to his house in California this summer. That night was my last night with Danny. I wished it would be endless.

After I returned his paper, Joseph studiously and conscientiously responded to my remarks comment by comment on his computer. If he wasn't sure what to do, he came into the English office and asked me. I would explain, and gradually we began to get to know each other. Through mostly simple editing and by cleaning up his usage and tenses, Joseph's paper became readable and he was able to get the credit he deserved.

In English class, some of the students called Joseph "The Computer," but I hoped Joseph's grade on his revision would help him begin to change this image. Still shy, he began to smile in class a little. "Things aren't as bad as last year," he told me. "I guess I'm not so lousy in English anymore."

As Joseph began to loosen up in class, we also started to see more of each other outside the classroom. Joseph would watch for me during our joint lunch periods. Finally, working up his nerve, he asked me to help him with his college essays. I answered Joseph the way I reply to all my seniors, "I'll conference with you, but you must bring drafts of your essays along."

At noon, Joseph kept sticking his head into the English office to report his progress. After a few weeks of revising his college essays on his computer and using his spellcheck and grammar programs, Joseph showed the drafts to me. "What do you think, Mrs. Lott?" he asked, grinning nervously.

I didn't know what to answer; Joseph's essays were impossible to understand. Dizzy, looking for focus, I followed his sentences as they went round and round on the page, never making a point outright. Finally, I pointed to the essay on top of the pile. "What are you trying to say here?" I asked. "Why was coming to America an important turning point in your life?"

Shyly, in stumbling fashion, he told me.

"But why didn't you write that on the paper?"

"It wouldn't be polite," he replied, looking down at the floor.

Puzzled, I asked Joseph what being polite had to do with coming to the point in a piece of writing. That's when he began to explain. "In Asia it's considered impolite and wrong to go straight to the point."

"I never knew that," I said, feeling more like the student than the teacher. "Traditionally, in America we teach people to be honest and straightforward. Did you ever hear the story of George Washington and the cherry tree?" Joseph shook his head.

Several questions and many explanations later, Joseph began to comprehend this apocryphal American tale, yet he still did not think that I understood him. "We're not taught to be dishonest, Mrs. Lott. It's just that we're supposed to circle the issue. In Asia, it's impolite to go right to the point."

Listening to Joseph explain while observing his shy, gentle manner, my mind turned to the Chinese poetry I had read, the poetic paintings I had seen. Truly, Joseph and I were involved in a cross-cultural dilemma. If Joseph wanted to be accepted into an American university, he would not only have to learn to write differently, he would also have to learn to think in another way, a way very different from how he had been taught in his own culture. It was particularly important that he change in order for him to write an expository essay that clearly made a point, the sort of essay that colleges were asking for. To this purpose, Joseph and I worked during many lunches while I repeated again and again, "What do you mean, Joseph? Then say it," and Joseph sat in front of the English department's computer revising and revising without eating a thing.

After much effort on both of our parts, Joseph mailed his essays off to colleges. "I want to be an executive with a large computer company," Joseph told me, "so I can make lots of money and have the latest equipment."

Still in high school, Joseph was working toward his goal. His efforts in science were outstanding. In addition, he had been selected as one of the student leaders to represent South Brunswick High School at the Apple computer conference. From my point of view as his English teacher, Joseph's computer knowledge helped him successfully revise his papers. Unfortunately, though, it was not until spring, when Joseph was still repeating the same incorrect usage, that I began to see his obsession with computers as a barrier that blocked him from learning English.

Joseph handed in his first journal as a computer printout and his second as a HyperCard stack. Even the cover pages of Joseph's papers were embellished with extravagant computer designs. Other students gave book reports, wrote poetry, or memorized soliloquies; Joseph presented talking HyperCard stacks. When a caricature of Joseph appeared under "Joseph Chang Productions," we asked in amazement, "How did you get your likeness into the computer?" "How did you get it to make that sound?" The class was impressed with Joseph's expertise, and so was I.

There were two problems, though, that I didn't see clearly at the time. First, Joseph was using his computer to avoid practicing language. Second, since I was impressed with Joseph's computer knowledge, I gave tacit approval to this behavior. Even when I assigned group projects, his group gladly gave Joseph the role of technology expert and he ended up in front of the computer alone. Protective of Joseph's shyness and wanting to encourage his strengths, I allowed these things to happen.

Certainly, I had observed students who did not feel as though they belonged, who withdrew from social situations. As far as I can remember, I had tried my best to include them in the classroom. Joseph's situation was unusual, though. He had an academically acceptable defense—his computer. But because school was one of the few places where Joseph could practice English—it was rarely spoken at home—he, even more than other shy students, needed to talk and listen. Instead, he immersed himself in computers. He seemed to trust them, to be comfortable with them, more so than with his peers.

Mostly, Joseph worked at his computer, revising his writing from my comments. In reflection, I must admit that I am not even sure how well Joseph read. I knew he read slowly; that he used a dictionary and that he stayed up past reasonable hours to complete his assignments. But Joseph rarely participated in class discussions. "I don't know how to say it," he would retort when I confronted him, and afraid to embarrass him, I would desist. Joseph's outside reading list at the end of senior year looked like this: *Minds and Tools*; *How to Get into College*; *HyperCards and Tricks*; *The Macintosh Bible*; and *Introduction to Computing*. Joseph lived, ate, and breathed technology. Computers responded to his diligence and intelligence. To Joseph, reading and communicating with his peers were less interesting and more complex.

Perhaps, too, there was an aspect of Joseph's obsession with computers that wasn't social in nature. Clearly, Joseph had a goal: to secure a high-paying job with a big computer company. Maybe the way to achieve his goal was, in fact, to be as single-minded as he had been, to value computer expertise over language acquisition. Joseph didn't have the luxury, as did some of my students, to become a liberal arts major, explore the humanities, and then think about a career. Maybe, given his choices, he needed to prove himself more than he needed to learn to speak and write conventional English.

In class, though, Joseph did begin to reveal a strength that wasn't entirely single minded. He wrote very good short stories. In fiction, he could express himself successfully in the Asian tradition, circling the issue, using metaphor, not going straight to the point. To me, Joseph's stories were an inspiration. Reading them, I realized that I should encourage more students to write in genres other than traditional essays. Fiction writing helped Joseph expand his thinking and understand his world. It also gave him the opportunity to experience success.

In one story, he hooked a "fifteen feet long blue marlin" that dragged him into the sea. After he was submerged, Joseph himself metamorphosized into a dolphin.

> I couldn't swim because my feet were pasted and wrapped around by a substance that I had never touched before. My arms were shrinking while my nose was growing. I continued to fall. . . . Suddenly, everything ceased to move. I knew I had reached the bottom; I had reached the continent down under.
>
> Everything down there was so different from the world I had been in. Unlike our old world, this whole continent was one completely united nation. There weren't any boundaries or dictatorships. Swimming around to find some friends could make me get used to this new environment very fast. . . . I became a good friend with a bass. . . . He told me not to go too deep because dolphins needed to breathe air on the surface. Despite of that I couldn't communicate with him well because of the difference in language, I started to feel like I was at home. . . .
>
> As the time passed by, I couldn't hold my breath any longer. I sprinted to the surface. A fish swam by and laughed at me. . . . I encountered a school of dolphins and shared the experience of being dolphins in a new world like this. They were all born in here. In a way, they made me look not as intelligent as they. They wanted me to join them, but I rejected their offer because the only friends they had were themselves. They made me look even more different from what I was because dolphins always stay in a group. . . . I wanted to be a fish more than a dolphin

because dolphins always need to go back to the surface of water to breathe. They don't really belong to this ocean. They are half dog and half fish. I wanted to be a one complete animal, not half of one. My philosophy for being a living organism was to fit into the surroundings. Unfortunately, I wouldn't be able to completely change what I was, but I would still try my best to accomplish this task.

Joseph wrote this short story, an allegory entitled "A Foreigner from the Surface," without any feedback from me. Creatively and imaginatively, he described in terms of metaphor what it felt like to descend into a foreign space, uncertain where he could survive, knowing that he wanted to belong. As difficult as it had been for me to begin to teach Joseph how to write an expository essay, fiction seemed to come naturally to him; he needed little instruction. In fact, when Joseph asked me proudly, "How do you like my ending, Mrs. Lott?" I was the one who needed to be enlightened. "Did you understand about the star at the end?" he wanted to know. Joseph's concluding paragraph went like this:

There was only dark from where I lived because it was so deep under from the surface. Up there, the bright side, all the dolphins stayed happily together. They still couldn't do what I had been practicing to do which was to develop the strength to hold my breath as long as I wanted. Now I stayed with the bass most of the time. One night while I lay down on the white sand talking to him, I looked up; I saw a little red star falling from the sky slowly, and it then gradually vanished into the dark. However, I didn't make a wish.

"What do you mean?" I answered, stalling for time.

"The star at the end of my story is the light on my father's boat that I described in the beginning. You know, while I was fishing with him, before I was pulled overboard. Did you get that?"

Turning to the first page of Joseph's fiction, I saw that he had, in fact, foreshadowed his conclusion. He had written, "Through that dark media, my dad's little boat might look like a lonely star to residents down there; and for them, I was an unknown." If Joseph's father's boat fell from the sky like a star, it, too, would descend below the surface, as would Joseph's father; then there would be no need for Joseph to make a wish.

Embarrassed, I did not confess to Joseph that I had missed this symbol. Before my experience with his paper, I had always thought of myself as a good reader. Joseph, though, was more adept at subtlety than I, his American teacher.

There was another symbol in "A Foreigner from the Surface," however, that was not so subtle: Asian technology. At the beginning of Joseph's short story, before the blue marlin pulled him down and he turned into a dolphin, he and his father were off the coast of Hong Kong, fishing from his father's boat.

> "Here, hold on to this." He handed me a spaceage material made rod with sophisticated craftsmanship around the golden gears inside its reel. The sun reflected from a little silver plate on the rod. Its brightness blasted through my pupils and marked "Made in Japan." His head slightly shook while his fingers were trying to tie a knob on the hook. He turned to me and confidently said, "There is no way the fish can escape from this Japanese made product." Like a pair of ordinary father and son figures, we liked to share our hobbies together, and so we started to fish.
>
> Fishing, a game or a fight that takes away a life through the ocean. The loot for the winner was the opponent's body without a soul. Through my father, fish are always the losers because of the invasion of Asian technology. . . .

According to Joseph's fiction, his father taught him that Americans were the fish who lived down under and that Asians, with their advanced technology, could seduce and catch them. With the mastery of this technology, Joseph believed he could be on top, the survivor, the conqueror — the fisherman.

As the year progressed, most of my interaction with Joseph outside of class revolved around computers. After years of lamenting how difficult it was to revise at home on my type-writer, I finally purchased a Macintosh SE with help from my parents. Joseph and my son Larry became my instructors, responding to my frantic phone calls and patiently talking me out of the mires in which I managed to get stuck. Joseph and I both enjoyed this role reversal, but it came about as a result of the invasion of Asian technology, just as his father had predicted.

Technology, though, didn't stand alone in a position of primacy for Joseph. When I asked him to evaluate my class at the end of the year, he wrote: "Another advantage of this class is that you give us enough time to conference with you about papers. What I like the best is the personal comments you give after grading each paper. They really influenced the way I approached to the next paper. . . . "

Writing conferences and personal comments were impor-tant to Joseph. In high school, cliques are established early. Newcomers who enter during their junior or senior year, like Joseph, often feel lonely and unsure of teacher expectations. And it was as useful for me to get to know Joseph as it was for him to feel comfortable with me.

When I reflect back on my experiences with Joseph, I feel proudest of his fiction writing. Each time he revised one of his short stories, he became a better writer. My intuition is that if I had been able to work with him longer, I would have been able to forge a connection between Joseph's fiction writ-ing and his expository essays. Even though my department believes otherwise, I see more similarities than differences among the genres. Joseph's hard work did pay off, though. He was accepted to several colleges of his choice. At the end of the year, I invited him to my home to celebrate. Always the computer whiz, he brought his disks with him to install some new programs on my Macintosh. It was not until later, when I used my newly installed HyperCard calendar, that I saw what Joseph had written. Conscientious as usual, he had inscribed at the end of each calendar week "Back up your hard drive!" Each time I do, I think of him.

A few months ago, between semesters at college, Joseph stopped by the English office. I couldn't help but notice that he appeared more relaxed.

"I passed English," he began, "with a B. My roommate helped me edit my papers." Joseph continued talking fluently, his face lit from within. "My roommate listens to classical music. We're good friends. When I'm by myself, I play Mozart and Bach."

As Joseph and I continued our conversation, I realized that he had not mentioned the word "computers." Joseph was changing. Living at college had helped expand his interests. He was becoming more assimilated into American culture. No longer a dolphin, Joseph had become "a special fish who could associate with bass."

Carol

Private, Keep Out

Carol, like many seventeen year olds, was uncertain of her identity and uncomfortable with certain people. Potentially a good writer, she was not able to develop her own work within the context of the classroom. With each draft, she lost more and more of what she originally intended to say.

I allowed a week for Carol and her classmates to write their autobiographical essays about a person who was important to them. During that time, I wrote myself, gave minilessons, encouraged freewriting, arranged writing groups, conferenced with students, and required drafting and peer editing. Although Carol didn't choose to conference with me, she wrote several drafts of her paper and conferenced with Denise, her peer editor.

In the beginning of the year, I usually allowed my classes to choose peer editors for their first pieces of writing. After all, since I didn't know their writing well, I was probably less qualified than they to match them appropriately. More often than not, friends paired up. This did not bother me; my friends also acted as peer editors for me outside of school. While students edited, I walked around the room, sitting down with one pair or another from time to time to solve problems.

Exchanging papers with each other, peer editors responded personally, commenting on what they liked or related to and discussing what was not clear or needed to be explained further. Depending on the particular assignment, peer editors were also instructed to look for evidence of what I had been teaching—an expanded conclusion, for instance. And finally, it was the responsibility of a peer editor to edit the paper before it was handed in for a grade. Trained in a procedure in which they put numbers on the paper that they were editing and responded on a separate sheet, editors were often graded. My purpose in doing this was to ensure that students took the task seriously. Some were excellent editors and/or cared about their friends and their editing grades. Others ended up giving little or no help; in some cases, a few even had a negative impact. This was the case with Denise and Carol.

Carol's essay "Salad Breaks," a skeleton of a piece, was the result of the week's activity. Typed, it filled less than half a page.

> Rebecca Anne Dombrawski was always dieting. I would come into the Physical Therapy Room for Ciped [a community-based program for juniors] only to find her munching on some variety of salad. Never will she be forgotten in my heart. Once, during one of her meetings, I walked in. She stopped everything and talked to me! The person she was talking to was a visiting therapist. He looked at her like she had purple hair, but she kept talking to me, and explaining the new procedure for treating pulled knees.
>
> Another time all of the therapists were talking about their favorite recipes, and out of the blue Rebecca asked me what I wanted to do as a career. I was in a state of shock! We had never discussed my future. It was not relevant, yet.
>
> Next Ciped day went fast. There were too many patients. As I was walking out the door I heard, "You should be a Physical Therapist." Since that day that has been my goal, not because Rebecca Anne said so, but because it's my dream. But it doesn't hurt that she said so, also.

All year Carol's editor Denise was an enigma. She sat in the right-hand corner of the room, between Carol, Stephanie, and two other friends, and one of the five girls always looked left out or unhappy. Most times, it was either Stephanie or Carol. And although Denise's comments to Carol on paper were perfectly supportive, I was uneasy with the dynamics even at the time.

49

Realizing as I reviewed the class's work that the rough draft upon which Denise had commented was fuller than Carol's final copy, I asked her, "Why did you make the decision to leave out so much? What happened when you were working with Denise? Do you want to talk about it?" Carol did not. It was not until June, though, in another context, that Carol talked about her need to keep her writing private. She told the class that she had kept a journal for six years, stored in the back of her closet. "I hate people to read my work," she said. "I can't stand it when they say something sucks."

Not until my sabbatical when I had time to speculate did I begin to question the formal procedure I called peer editing. Reflecting on my own writing process, I realized that my actions were different from my expectations for my students. First of all, I didn't show everything I wrote to peers for comments. I selected what I wanted friends to look at and also the stage at which I asked for their response. If something was to be published, I was usually anxious for feedback. Otherwise, if I were writing for myself or for another individual or a small group, I often did not solicit comments. Furthermore, I felt flattered when friends asked me to respond to their work — not only because they valued my opinion, but also because they trusted me. Even so, sometimes I refused if I had a deadline of my own. Rarely did my friends and I exchange work simultaneously, nor did we need a greater reward than hearing from each other that our opinions mattered. In institutionalizing this friendly, voluntary process and rewarding it with a grade, I had somehow gotten off track.

My own written comments on Carol's paper were meant to be supportive and nonthreatening: "Is the reader going to know what Ciped is?" I asked. "What was the meeting about?" "What room was it in?" "Why did you walk in?" "Can you describe Rebecca? "What did she actually say?" "Do you want to use dialogue?" And although Carol answered some of these questions in her revision, it was still as though only part of her was speaking.

In Carol's next paper, a film analysis of *The Graduate*, the same thing happened. She and Denise insisted upon working together, even though this time I questioned their choice. "There's no problem; Denise helps me," Carol remonstrated. But, after I collected the papers, once again I saw that Carol had started out with a good idea, became frightened along the way, and had stopped writing. She wanted to demonstrate that Ben was attracted to Mrs. Robinson because she was similar to his mother. Her second and third paragraphs follow:

> As the film begins, Benjamin is in an airport on a moving walk; he is staring off into space. There are signs and posters behind him. One says, in huge boldface letters, "Make sure it matches." This sign refers to matching luggage, but I think Nichols is also trying to foreshadow the similarities between Mrs. Braddock (Elizabeth Wilson) and Mrs. Robinson (Ann Bancroft).
>   Throughout the film, Nichols shows both Mrs. Robinson and Mrs. Braddock as sexy. In one scene particularly Nichols shows Mrs. Braddock almost as if she is a seductress. She slithers into the steam-filled bathroom scantily dressed in a long, silk nightgown and robe that are half falling off her thin but muscular frame. Ben is standing in his boxer shorts cautiously shaving as if to scrape the thoughts of his mother away, slowly.

Both of these paragraphs were well written with original insights. I particularly enjoyed the alliteration of S's in the second paragraph and the way Carol played with the metaphor of Ben's razor as he "scrape[d] the thoughts of his mother away, slowly." Carol was a good writer, but beyond these two paragraphs all she produced for her final draft was a four-line introduction and a five-line conclusion. Unlike Rahul, whose writing on the same subject had been inflated, Carol's was brief to a fault. And even though in her film analysis, Carol was not asked to write about herself, each progressive draft became shorter and shorter.

Revising to Carol seemed to mean crossing out. And since her revision was final, according to my tenets at the time, I missed an opportunity to work with her on expanding her ideas. Instead, I tackled the issue of Carol's spare writing in a more general way.

At my invitation, Carol and I met for lunch in October in an empty classroom to discuss the problem. Although Carol appeared outgoing, almost boisterous, in class, in this rather intimate situation, she looked far from relaxed. I tried to put her at ease by chatting about things that were happening at school. Finally, I asked, "What do you think the problem is with your writing?"

Ignoring the question, she replied, "My father's interested in African history." I nodded. "He teaches my brother and me. He gets up two hours before work and reads and studies," she continued. "Two weekends ago he attended a conference and stayed up all night talking."

In a friendly fashion, I inquired, "What does your mother do?"

"She's an operating room nurse," Carol answered. "She loves blood and guts. She commutes to New York three days a week, and the rest of the time she sleeps. We're not allowed to disturb her."

"So why do you have so much trouble getting words on paper?" I continued, attempting to refocus the discussion.

"My best friend, Martha Manning, is really upset," she rejoined. "I'm from the Midwest, you know. We care about our friends there; I just can't help it."

I didn't know what else to say. Carol was obviously trying to tell me something, but for the life of me—at the time—I could not figure out what. A few assignments later, Carol's problem became clearer.

Right now I'm acting and being everyone but the self that belongs to me. I'm Sharon, quiet, and Suzanne, with laughing eyes, but they aren't me. A friend of mine was told his grandfather is dying of cancer, and he's leaving tomorrow. I'm fleeing because I don't want to face the reality that my best friend is leaving. There won't be a person left I have complete confidence in—to tell and discover my problems and feelings. I'm really hurting while writing, because in order to write this I am myself, not another. For these ten minutes I am the self I'd love to escape from. Well, now I'm leaving myself. I think I'll leave my feelings here in myself and be Denise. I'll wear a mask that I'm just quiet and don't feel like talking. As Denise's self, I feel nothing. It's better that way.

Carol shared this journal entry with the class, furtively looking up at me while she read aloud. It was January, and Carol was still having trouble writing. Her highest grade on a paper had been a C–, but most of her grades fell even lower. She edited herself out before she picked up a pen, and when she did manage to cover a page or two for a rough draft, as soon as her peer editor— no matter who she or he was—made a comment, she lost all confidence in what she had written. The sparseness of her final writing was such that there was little on which to comment. I resorted to filling the spaces with questions. But in a journal writing that was not to be critiqued, Carol, similar to Rahul, had begun to reveal herself.

Carol's next piece of writing in was a poem composed outside of school. Presenting it orally to the class, she looked around the room proudly, aware of her accomplishment.

Randall and I — Lost

I'm trying to figure out
what makes me tick
It's a very simple plan
But there's just a little bug in it, ya see
Sometimes if I'm hiding inside a mask
I get lost
The mask I portray and my real self
get mixed together (intertwine)
So I can't tell who or what I am
I can't just drop the mask

'Cause then people would see the real me
And the real me isn't very pretty
Besides, I'm not gettin' hurt again
So forget you

With your goodygoody advice
About being a phoney
My mask suits me fine
Even if I do get lost

In class, we had just finished reading a play written in the sixties by William Hanley called *Slow Dance on the Killing Ground*. The play dealt with two characters who had made disastrous choices in their lives and one who was about to. Carol's favorite character was Randall, an African-American man growing up in New York City with a genius-level IQ, who masked his intelligence in order to survive. During the night in which the play is set and unknown to the two other characters until the final scene, Randall killed his mother in response to emotional injuries she had inflicted on him. Not only did Carol volunteer to play the part of Randall when we performed the play in class, but she also wrote the above poem as part of her final project.

Several aspects of Carol's final project attracted my attention. First of all, left to her own devices, she had chosen to write a poem. Poetry by its very nature is spare, similar to the papers that Carol had turned in. Was she showing me that poetry, a genre in which I had given her little opportunity to write, was her style of preference?

Secondly, this play had interested her more than other works studied in the course. In my own commitment to process writing, I had forgotten the importance of involvement. With Carol, I had not taken into consideration her commitment to the material. Steps in the writing process can be empty motions if a student does not care about her paper—if she is insecure about herself or unwilling to defend her thoughts to peers.

And thirdly, her poem had been written at home without the requirements of formalized drafting and editing. In her previous papers, Carol had performed empty motions. Insecure about herself and uninvolved with her material, she had been intimidated by peer commenting. At this point in her development, Carol's "mask" was most important to her. As she wrote in her poem, she couldn't "just drop the mask/ 'Cause then people would see the real me/ And the real me isn't very pretty/ Besides, I'm not gettin' hurt again." As she herself said, her "mask suits [her] fine/ Even if [she does] get lost."

In the second semester, however, there was somewhat of a breakthrough. We had been reading Kafka's *Metamorphosis*, and in February I invited my class to write a short piece of fiction in which they, too, metamorphosized into something other than another human being. Carol enjoyed this assignment, perhaps because she transformed herself into a dragon, or perhaps because, as I had been noticing, she did better in fictive and poetic modes.

> I snapped and turned to walk away. As my back faced her, she grabbed my shoulder and held it, giving me no choice but to look at her. I stiffened and arched my back as if I were a provoked cat. I hissed. But instead of air and saliva smelling of breakfast and tic tacs, I breathed fire. Marveling at the changing colors of her hair I had set aflame, I walked away.

In Carol's original draft, which once again had gone through the writing process in class (this time without Denise) she had had her same old problems. When I gave back the papers in class, though, I asked, "How can you help somebody who has trouble getting her thoughts out on paper?" The students had good suggestions: "Pretend you're not writing a paper for school." "Write out all your thoughts even if they don't go together." "Figure out a way that you, personally, connect to the topic." I only glanced at Carol, but when I handed back her paper, I casually asked if any of their suggestions were good ones. "Maybe you should pretend you're not writing the paper," I told her. Carol gave me a huge smile. "I think that will work," she said.

Another difference, and perhaps a second reason for her breakthrough, was in my commenting. On this paper, I made fewer comments than I had on previous ones, complimented her ending, and finished in a general fashion with, "Carol, this has real potential. Your big problem is how you handle your transformations from woman to dragon and back again. How did the woman get out of her dragon-self to get to school in the last scene?"

When Carol handed me her revision, she looked more at ease than she had in the past, jiggling around my desk as I put the papers in a folder. "How'd you do? Do you like your story?" I asked. "I like it," she answered with a mischievous smile. "I think I pretty much wrote what I wanted to say." I thought she did, too. Carol's paper rated a B+ with this comment: "You're really sounding like *yourself* now."

During February, March, and April, Carol wrote. No longer having a problem covering a page as she had in the beginning of the year, she was more self-confident. Her grades, however, did not improve. At the time, I attributed this to end of the year senioritis or simple laziness. In Carol's analysis of *Who's Afraid of Virginia Woolf?*, for example, there were incorrect details. Few of her ideas were supported with examples or quotations from the text. Although Carol was now more at ease writing, it looked to me as though she had not even studied the play.

Now, as I read over her self-evaluation of this paper, I think my own analysis might have been too simplistic. In answer to the question, "What are the strengths of my paper?" Carol wrote, "I'm not very confident with this paper, because it wasn't an assignment I was very interested in. My best paper, I feel, was my metamorphosis one because I actually had the desire to work on it." And again, her answer to the question, "What three things do you like best in this paper?" was "I don't really like anything about this paper. It wasn't an assignment I enjoyed."

Could Carol have disliked analyzing *Who's Afraid of Virginia Woolf?* because Albee's play involved middle-aged whites arguing? I knew she liked drama; I remembered how involved she had been with Hanley's play. Perhaps the problem with

Carol's paper had been more than end-of-the-year senioritis. Nevertheless, it was my responsibility to grade her fairly. Although a better grade could have encouraged her, it would have been unrealistic. Caught in the undercurrent of high school procedure, I didn't stop and think. Today I would be more cautious and grade less often, knowing that grades are probably the strongest message we give to students.

In Carol's subsequent papers, there were further problems, many of which I attributed to her carelessness. Commenting more and more, I tried to justify the grades I gave her. Yet, as I look over these papers now, I can see progress. Although Carol's work was not at the level it should have been at the end of a senior academic course, she certainly had come a long way from that writer who could not cover half a page. Sadly, as I look over one of Carol's last self-evaluations, I realize the injustice I did her. "What did you try to improve or experiment with on this paper?" Carol answered, "I could not even tell you my brain is so fried." "What are your questions about what you were trying to do?" "Did I do better on this paper or is it crappy like my others?" was Carol's poignant reply.

Ironically, I had spent the first half of the year getting Carol to write and the second half of the year criticizing her writing. It should have been no surprise to me — that although it was in May — Carol began to show the symptoms of skeletal writing once again. At the time, I threw up my hands, unable to recognize my own culpability.

Although I didn't help Carol as much as I might have, her story is important to me. As a writer myself, I know how central it is to be sure about who I am before I write. When I am uncomfortable or uncertain, my thinking is unclear. Also, much as I assiduously solicit comments on my writing, I only garner them from those whom I respect and trust. Even though Denise remained an enigma, the evidence of her influence on Carol was negative. Would Carol, because of her passion for privacy, have benefited more from an approach that did not involve peer editing? Reflecting on this in hindsight, I think so. She may not yet have been ready to discover in a public way what she had to say. Commenting and editing to her might have been counterproductive.

And there are other pedagogical considerations. Judging from Carol's differing degree of involvement with Hanley's and Albee's plays, it was evident that she did better when she was more sympathetic to what we were studying. Her interests should have been taken into consideration. Finally, if I had assessed Carol on her progress rather than on individual papers, her grades would have been higher. Assessing her the way I did eventually eroded the confidence I had worked so hard to instill.

Yet Carol is not very different from many other high school students. Insecure about her identity, she protected her privacy with a passion, played a passive/aggressive game of rebelling in school, and dared teachers to interest her in anything. Although I wish I had been able to teach her to develop her writing more effectively, in telling her story, I realize that some of the dynamics were beyond my control. As Carol matures, many of her problems may solve themselves.

Reflections

*I*n all three of the previous stories, I found that some of the materials and techniques I used in my classroom were culturally inappropriate. It was not fair for me to grade Rahul on his interpretation of *The Graduate*, nor was it particularly relevant for Carol to analyze *Who's Afraid of Virginia Woolf?*. Furthermore, with Joseph, Rahul, and Carol the process approach to writing, with an emphasis on peer editing as I had taught it, was fruitless. Joseph, because of his skill level, was never able to edit his partner's work. And it was just as uncomfortable for Carol and Rahul. None of us, when we feel as though we might be different, want to expose ourselves to what could be ridicule.

Other problems existed in the way I approached process writing in my classroom. As a writer, I knew that my own process was recursive and rarely the same from piece to piece. I ignored this knowledge, however. In order to simplify procedures and keep up with paperwork, I had turned writing into a lockstep formula. Every paper my students handed in, except for in-class tests, was attached to a rough draft and a peer editing sheet. It was not until I began to reflect on my teaching that I fully realized the futility of commenting on and assessing these "final copies."

Recognition of writing as a process has been an important step in the teaching of writing. Even so, we must continue to question. John Holt, in a journal entry from 1958, that was later published in his book *How Children Fail* (1964), wrote about classroom procedures in general:

We need to ask more often of everything we do in school, "Where are we trying to get, and is this thing we are doing helping us to get there?" Do we do something because we want to help the children and can see that what we are doing is helping them? Or do we do it because it is inexpensive or convenient for school, teachers, administrators? Or because everyone else does it? We must beware of making a virtue of necessity, and cooking up high-sounding educational reasons for doing what is done really for reasons of administrative economy or convenience. The still greater danger is that, having started to do something for good enough reasons, we may go on doing it stubbornly and blindly.

Process writing and peer editing were introduced into the schools for good reasons. But as John Holt said more than thirty years ago, it would be a danger to stop asking questions and to follow rote procedure.

Although it is easier to blame the system, upon reflection I now realize that the endings of some of these stories were not within my control. Joseph, for example, needed more individual attention as well as a class in expository writing and work with a reading specialist. Because I had five large classes, a full schedule, and an established curriculum, my frustration was inevitable. Setbacks were almost as unavoidable with Carol. Perhaps I could have changed myself and my commitment to the writing process in order to work more effectively with her, but I tend to hold on to what I believe in, even when there's evidence that it's impractical to do so.

Yet even in these three stories, there *were* things I did that were successful, such as journal writing—writing where the self, rather than the teacher, was the primary audience. In their journals, Rahul and Carol began to talk. Toby Fulwiler (1985) suggests that journal writing works because when students write in their journals, they individualize instruction. The act of unevaluated silent writing to generate ideas, make observations, or become aware of emotions, is a personal one. Even when journal writing takes place in the classroom, it is a private exploration. Thus, journal writing seems somewhat removed from the school environment.

Not only were journals a way for these students to connect to their writing, but also they provided a medium for me to understand our interactions better. Reading students' journals kept me in touch with students, making me more aware of their individual needs. Journal writing and/or in-class writing also figured in these stories as an effective method to get juices flowing. It dovetailed with my desire for more ungraded, private writing in the high school classroom. Although journals initially may have seemed like one extra project in an already busy teaching schedule, now I cannot think of a more efficient resource.

Requiring different writing forms was also helpful. Carol's poetry affected her prose in a positive manner. She began to develop a facility to play with language. And Joseph could say in fiction what he could not express, at that time, in essays. Although it would be satisfying if all high school students learned to write well in every mode, we have to take into consideration their experience and what they have in fact read.

Ultimately, though, the most important conclusion I came to after reflecting on my work with Rahul, Joseph, and Carol, was that color and cultural background cannot be ignored. Initially, I had worked with these three students as though I were color-blind. Mike Rose (1989), in his moving account of his own teaching, eloquently discusses the harm that can result from this:

> To have any prayer of success [in educating a pluralistic society], we'll need many conceptual blessings: A philosophy of language and literacy that affirms the diverse sources of linguistic competence and deepens our understanding of the ways class and culture blind us to the richness of those sources.... We'll need a pedagogy that encourages us to step back and consider the threat of the standard classroom and that shows us, having stepped back, how to step forward to invite a student across the boundaries of that powerful room. Finally, we'll need a revised store of images of educational excellence, ones closer to egalitarian ideals — ones that embody the reward and turmoil of education in a democracy, that celebrate the plural, messy human reality of it.

Thinking of myself as an idealist, I had not sufficiently recognized "the plural, messy human reality" of the classroom.

I found that pretending all students respond alike, no matter what their backgrounds, is an unrewarding game for everyone involved. And if my naivete was the result of the fact that I am a white American, that difficulty has been compounded by the complexion of our English department, which is decidedly white except for Doris, an African-American woman who was hired only three years ago. I realize now that Doris and I should stop acting as though cultural differences do not exist and begin a serious discussion about those that do.

Two years ago, a group of black parents, concerned that the needs of their sons and daughters were not being met, asked for a meeting with Richard Kaye, our principal. Richard listened sympathetically to their complaints and then held a series of discussions with students from various cultures. For the English department, one result of these dialogues was the purchase of world literature texts to be studied senior year. Although an excellent start, textbooks did not turn out to be the complete answer. Teachers were not sufficiently prepared to teach them. Looking for help, we saw that many schools were having similiar problems. After attending two workshops on multicultural issues, I realized that the richest resource for me was my students. They knew more about their own diverse cultures than I did. They just had to be asked.

Part Three

Revealing the Complexities

When we ask students to think about language separately from what they mean to say, we ask them to perform tasks working writers would never perform—sentences aren't simply syntactic patterns diagrammed on a page, and no one composes by blueprint.

— Robert L. Root, Jr.

Jane

A Space of Her Own

*J*ane relished ideas, often looking at them from several perspectives. She was rarely the first to speak in a discussion, listening carefully instead. I liked to watch her face when she did this. I could almost see thoughts move across her forehead. When Jane did speak, usually right before the end of class, she had synthesized what had gone on, enlarged on it, and then reshaped it with her own ideas.

And yet, Jane didn't seem to be able to do this on paper. She had been recommended for Honors English all through high school, but she rarely achieved A's. English was not the only subject where this happened. Several months after we came to know one another, Jane told me about her history term paper. She had organized it as her teacher taught her, writing down a thesis and researching material to support it. As Jane had neared the end of her paper, she had begun to see things differently, realizing that the opposite of her thesis might be true. She had ended up refuting her thesis in the last few pages of her paper, failing the history department's objective of creating a strong argument.

Jane's writing never seemed to crystallize. It was either unfocused, as in her history term paper, or it was flat and one dimensional, as in her English papers. For example, this introductory paragraph:

Essay #1: In "Antigone," a tragedy by Sophocles, Creon, the king of Thebes, is not the tragic hero of the play. He does not fully fit the definition of a tragic hero, stated above, as it is cited from the textbook, *Western Literature*, edited by Robert Carlsen. Therefore, he cannot be a tragic hero.

The first quality defining a tragic hero is, "a tragic hero must be a man or a woman capable of great suffering." It can be shown with the following situation and quotes that Creon is not capable of suffering.

This essay had turned up in a folder later when a colleague of mine cleared out her files. "Do you think Jane might want these?" she asked me. Curiously, I looked to see what Jane had written junior year. None of the writing reflected Jane as I knew her.

Oddly enough, I had been given a clue to this absence of "Jane" from her writing in one of her senior papers.

Sitting silently in the darkness behind the closed door, I listened as my brother and sister walked around my room trying to find me.

The closet was my favorite place growing up and continues to be now. Its dark and silent privacy was a place I often ran to when I needed to be alone. Even now, when I want some undisturbed time to think I sometimes crawl in.

Leaning up against the wall, behind the overstuffed rack of clothes, I was sheltered from the rest of the world. In the wintertime I wrapped myself in my green and yellow afghan like a caterpillar in a cocoon. In the warmth I began to grow as I sorted out my problems and concerns. The dull and muted shadows reassured me that I could reveal my deepest thoughts without fear of others seeing what I was feeling.

Jane was not in the habit of telling others her thoughts and feelings, nor was she in the habit of writing them down. She had had little experience revealing herself on paper. One might say that she closeted her complete self. But these insights came later. While I was teaching Jane, I worked intuitively, not consciously aware of what might be holding her back.

For her first English paper in September, Jane described Harry Schultz, a colleague of mine. He had never taught Jane, but he had played the part of Tevye opposite her Hodel in *Fiddler on the Roof.* Harry was chosen as "the person who was important in her life." Jane had a complication to deal with though, since she had only met Harry three days before opening night. Jane had been an understudy and had not played Hodel in rehearsal until then. One might very well ask how Harry had influenced her in so short a time. The final paragraphs of Jane's paper reveal this:

> The day of opening night finally arrived and he handed me a card. I opened the envelope carefully and curiously. As I opened the card a beautiful gold necklace and butterfly pendant fell out into my lap. I picked it up and looked at it in wonder, feeling flattered and special. I went on to read the message on the card. He wrote, "I've given all my stage family necklaces which belonged to my late wife Sandy—because of a dream I had. This one is for you. Come out of your cocoon and share the beauty of your generosity and feelings. Thanks for all you've done."
>
> Mr. Schultz and I were never very close. In fact, we had rarely ever talked. Yet he gave me something that was very special to him, that touched me in an indescribable way.
>
> Giving is easy when you know that you'll get something back in return. But Mr. Schultz taught me about what giving truly means.

As excellent as Jane's final paragraphs were, there were still some problems with her essay as a whole, mainly because she had oversimplified her relationship with Harry. It was not clear whether his gift was a sentimental gesture or if, in some way, he and Jane did know each other. My comment to Jane on her final paper was, "You take suggestions beautifully; you've handled everything we've conferenced in class about well. I particularly like the way you wrote about opening Mr. S's card. It's almost there. But your relationship with Mr. Schultz still isn't clear."

When I handed back the papers and Jane looked at my comments, she challenged me by blurting, "I'm not changing it. I like it the way it is." I nodded an okay, unsure just how to work with her.

Unexpectedly, Jane came to the English office three days later during my prep period without having made an appointment. We talked for about fifteen or twenty minutes, but never about her paper or her writing. Instead, we talked about the complications of Jane's relationship with Harry. She did not really know him. What did he mean to her? Jane came back again two days later during my lunch period, and we continued our dialogue in the same way. Jane used me as a sounding board, analyzing her feelings, cracking open the door to her closet inch by inch. After our second conference, Jane revised her paper, leaving her final paragraphs unchanged. She now understood what Harry meant to her, as her third paragraph shows.

> It was that night that I first worked closely with Mr. Schultz. We had been at rehearsals together for three months, yet we had never really talked. For me Mr. Schultz was a man of legend. Many of my friends had had him as an English teacher. They talked about Mr. Schultz with endless praise. They said how much they loved how he made learning fun, and how his sometimes brutally honest comments made them laugh. Other friends held him as their idol. I had seen Mr. Schultz's incredible acting ability, but for me he hadn't become real until that night at rehearsal. It was then that something between us clicked. We began as two individuals who barely knew each other, but before the night was over we became our characters. Mr. Schultz and I, as Tevye and Hodel, became close. Unfortunately though, Mr. Schultz and I never got to know each other.

This became our conference style. Stealthily, after a paper was assigned, Jane would appear in the English office unannounced, needing a sounding board. Sometimes I was available for conferencing; other times I was teaching or working with another student. Conference after conference, I was astounded by the amount of knowledge Jane processed. I began to call her thoughts "the trees" since she saw so many details and permutations that it was difficult for her to step back and see "the forest" unless we talked. Sometimes Jane worked too hard on a paper, trying to organize all her ideas without stepping back and seeing the bigger picture at all or until it was almost too late to have enough time to revise before the paper's due date, which may have been what had happened with her history term paper.

The process that Jane would go through before she wrote her essay on *A Streetcar Named Desire* shows her thinking/writing style clearly. Toward the end of the year, while we were discussing the play in class, I stopped and asked the students to write for five or ten minutes about why the gaudy paper lantern that Blanche bought on Bourbon Street to put over Stella and Stanley's bare light bulb was a metaphor for Blanche herself. Jane raised her hand and asked if she could list the reasons instead of writing a paragraph. When I gave her permission, she listed ten different points—all of them complex. Here are seven of them as she wrote them down.

- her having to shade her feeling—lies to cover her insecurity (nakedness)
- adorable little front—the lace and frills she puts on to hide behind
- she doesn't like bluntness—she plays with her words and gestures—infers a lot
- the lantern is paper—is destructable—her front is destructable
- she likes subtleness—and seems to enjoy some practicality in people. (Stella, Mitch) not the "raw material"
- Bourbon—that's interesting! Her "drinking"
- doesn't like bright lights on her because they hurt her appearance—yet she seems to like the spotlight

Jane's ideas came fast and some of them did not seem to follow in what, to me, was a natural sequence. An example is "she likes subtleness—and seems to enjoy some practicality in people." I see these characteristics as opposite, but obviously Jane's thinking does not follow the same pattern that mine does. Her next to last item—"Bourbon—that's interesting! Her 'drinking'" seems to have nothing to do with the items that she had listed before and after it.

Jane's chaotic listing, though, played a part in her prewriting for her final paper. Our after-school conference, which occurred a week before her paper was due, was slightly different from some of the earlier ones. Having made an appointment with me for a change, Jane paged through her notebook. Then, she began to talk about her ideas and not what she had actually written down. The conference went something like this:

JANE: I want to talk about reality and illusion in *Streetcar Named Desire*. I did some freewriting, but I don't know what form you want for the paper.

ME: What do you mean?

JANE: Well, I don't know if you want me to discuss it or you want me to have a thesis.

ME: What would the difference be?

JANE: Well, if I have to have a thesis I can compare Blanche in *Streetcar* to Amanda in *The Glass Menagerie*.

ME: Do you want to do that?

JANE: No, not really. They both lived in a world of illusion. I'd just list their similarities and their differences. It would be too "Mickey Mouse."

ME: What do you want to write about?

JANE: The way I see it, Blanche lives in a world of illusion—that's her reality. And when Stanley destroys her illusions, she's in reality, but reality is really an illusion to her. See, I told you. It's too complicated.

ME: No, it really sounds interesting. I guess we're all that way to some extent. I have some illusions I can't live without. But what about *The Glass Menagerie*?

JANE: Well, I haven't read it since sophomore year, but I kept a journal about it then. I think that there's a connection between Amanda and Blanche and that it has to do with Tennessee Williams' ideas about illusion and reality. Can you get me a book? I want to read it again tonight.

ME: Amanda? She raised two children on her own. She was a lot stronger than Blanche. What about Laura?

JANE: [So involved in her own idea she didn't hear me.] Can you do that? Can you say that a writer has certain ideas about illusion and reality from just reading his plays?

ME: Why not? He's dead. His plays are what's alive. Just make sure, though, that you can document what you're saying with material from the plays.

JANE: Of course.

ME: I'll get you a book.

Jane's subsequent essay became a significant step forward. Her introduction, compared to the single, formulaic paragraph she had written to introduce her *Antigone* paper demonstrates this growth.

> *"The pure and simple truth is rarely pure and never simple."*
> —Oscar Wilde

Such paradoxes are present in our everyday life. Things that at first glance seem simple and clear-cut, upon further examination transform their clear-cut, symmetrical edges into many faceted and complicated patterns. Tennessee Williams in his two plays, *A Streetcar Named Desire* and *The Glass Menagerie*, presents and discusses such a paradox, one of reality and illusion.

His characters live in a world of illusion they create for themselves in order to escape the real world which they feel they can't survive in. Yet, this world of illusion eventually becomes their reality and the real world becomes an illusion to them.

By most it is viewed unhealthy and harmful to live in a world of illusion formed to shelter people from the real world. But for a few, as Tennessee Williams shows us in his characters of Amanda in *The Glass Menagerie* and Blanche in *A Streetcar Named Desire*, it is more harmful to live in the real world and face reality than to live in their worlds of illusion.

For the first time, Jane's writing crystallized. Her paper was focused; she supported her ideas well; and at the same time, she revealed the complexity of her thinking. In answer to the question on her self-evaluation "What three things do you like best in this paper?" Jane wrote, "I like the intro. I like the skill of using metaphors. I think I worked hard on the paper so I'm just happy with my overall results."

Jane did work hard on her paper. In her self-evaluation, she said that she spent about fifteen hours on it. And when she submitted it, she told me, "I just lost track of time. First, I had to read *The Glass Menagerie* again. Then I sat in my room and just thought about it—I don't know how long." She showed me her notebook, one of those black marbelized ones with sewn-in pages, half of which were written on. "These are my drafts," Jane continued. "I wrote in it all week. I'd sit in the back of the room in my classes and whenever I got bored, I worked on it. It was always on my mind."

The compartmentalized structure of high school usually does not allow students to pursue their ideas for more than forty minutes at a stretch. I often wonder how I would fare in high school as the person I am today. When I work on a piece of writing that I care about, I find it difficult to fully attend to anything else. In some ways, Jane's previous writing had been the result of the artificial, fragmented atmosphere in which she had been forced to learn.

I was particularly gratified to see that by the end of senior year Jane was able to include the complexities of her thinking process in her writing without conferencing. For the final exam, I asked my students to write about a book that in some way had altered their views or opinions. Jane wrote about two: Chinua Achebe's *Things Fall Apart* and Maya Angelou's *I Know Why the Caged Bird Sings*. She wrote about both these books as "diffusing prejudice and leading to a more understanding, peaceful world." But Jane did not simplify her ideas in the process of doing this. Some of her thoughts on Angelou's autobiography follow:

> I identified with many of the main character, Maya's, emotions and attitudes toward life. However, because I am a white, middle-class teen reading in the 1990's about a poor, black girl who lived in the 1950's, I found some events in the book hard to understand. One of these things is the emphasis on God and the church. Although I am a practicing Catholic, I live in a society where there is little importance placed on religion, so it is hard to understand this concept which is present in both this book and in *Things Fall Apart*. I was also disturbed by the fact that in the South a black could be hunted down and killed just because of his color and the fact that he was in the wrong place at the wrong

time. The fear that Maya and the people in her town had of this was very real to them, but as a white who is relatively protected, this fear seems foreign to me.

Reading this book helped me to better relate to their bitterness towards my race, the whites, and showed me the hardships the blacks had to endure. However, reading this book was both a positive and a negative experience for me. I became more aware of the history and background of the black race which was positive, but I also became more quick to recognize and be aware of a black person's color.

It seems as though nothing that Jane thinks about is simply positive or negative. Reading I *Know Why the Caged Bird Sings* expanded Jane's vision and helped her to understand why blacks might feel the way they do toward whites. Yet, at the same time, Jane realized that the book made her more aware of color and of ways in which her experience as a white female was different than the experience of many blacks.

Back in September, Jane had revealed that a freshman year teacher had told her to write simple sentences: "Your papers are composed of run-ons." Jane had taken that teacher's advice seriously. But her interpretation of that advice began to inhibit her from writing about things in the complex way she truly looked at life.

How was I, her senior teacher, able to help her? The conference in preparation for Jane's paper on *A Streetcar Named Desire* demonstrates the intuitive nature of my relationship with Jane. When I reread our dialogue, it does not make a whole lot of sense as an instructional model. It was in the spaces, not in the words, that Jane formulated her ideas. Jane needed those spaces, places where she could hear herself think and begin to make sense of her own ideas. She needed to let out the richness she kept hidden inside.

Jane was a hard worker. She ultimately turned into an excellent student. My task as teacher was easier than it had been with many of her classmates. Jane knew where the commas went. She rarely misspelled words. All her paragraphs were connected by transitions. Each of her essays had an introduction, a body, and a conclusion. My main job with Jane turned out to be making myself available and open to her concerns from time to time. As a listener, I let Jane know that it was okay to reveal ideas. Not anxious for her to organize her thinking too quickly, I reassured her that thoughts rarely appear in neat little packages.

I would have liked to have given Jane other assurances: longer occasions during the high school day in which to write, dependable times for drop-in conferencing, and some continuity across the curriculum so that she wouldn't have had to hide herself in the back of a classroom when she wanted to pursue her ideas. But the environment of the public high school had been structured long before Jane and I met each other in room C102. We worked together the best we could.

Stephanie

A Cinderella Story

I was hurrying down the hall to the teachers' bathroom. A young woman rushed toward me, a wide smile on her face. "Mrs. Lott," she called, "I've been looking for you."

It was January, between semesters at most colleges. I knew she must be a former student. But, for the life of me, I could not remember who. Hesitantly, I tried "Stephanie." She smiled. We gave each other a hug. I remembered her.

"Don't worry about not recognizing me. I know I look different," she said with confidence. "I've lost thirty pounds and even have a boyfriend now, named Stephen. Pretty funny coincidence, huh? We met in line the first day at registration, kidding each other about our names."

Laughing, I asked, "How's Ohio?"

"Great! I got a 12 on my entrance writing exam and placed in Honors English."

Amazed, I managed to blurt out, "Congratulations! How'd you do first semester?"

"I got an A, Mrs. Lott. That's what I came to tell you."

I shouldn't have been surprised. Having taught Stephanie for two years—as a sophomore and then again as a senior—I knew her determination. Stephanie had made progress over the years. Somehow, though, I couldn't forget my English teacher hang-ups: the way Stephanie spelled, the way she flung commas on her papers like darts, the emotional way she presented her arguments, sometimes ignoring reason.

If I had reminisced a little longer, I would have recalled that the previous June Stephanie had shown me an A history paper, along with Mr. Guthrie's comment of "Who's your English teacher? This is very well organized." Both Stephanie and I had been flattered, but still . . . an A in Honors English?

It was not until my drive home that I had time to think about Stephanie. When I first met her in her sophomore year, I couldn't have predicted such success. Fifteen-year-old Stephanie was quite different from the attractive, self-assured young woman I had just seen.

One of the things I remember, besides her scrawling handwriting and run-on sentences, was Stephanie's coming up after class to ask me if I knew her brother. When I said I didn't, she replied, "He's in college now. I wondered if you'd heard of him. He's the smart one."

Even so, when we read *Catcher in the Rye* sophomore year, Stephanie's insights often kept the discussion going. Stephanie perceived and understood aspects of Holden Caulfield's adolescent behavior that many of her classmates ignored. By the time we finished Salinger's novel, I was referring to her as "Dr. Stephanie" in class, eliciting her "professional" opinion when other students were stymied. Nevertheless, Stephanie's papers sophomore year remained disappointing. "I can never write what I'm thinking," she complained each time I worked with her. "I have it up here," she'd say, pointing to her forehead, "but I can never get it out on paper."

We were happy to see each other again when her senior year rolled around. "Dr. Stephanie," I repeated, both of us smiling as I read the roll. Stephanie cried, however, as I handed back her first senior paper. This was an autobiographical essay about her grandfather, a person who had influenced her. Waiting for the class to leave before confronting me about her grade, she began in an angry fashion. "I don't deserve this. I worked so hard!"

"I know you've worked hard, but it's my job to prepare you for college," I retorted, frustrated with my responsibility. Handing her a tissue, I asked, "Would you like to revise your paper?" Sobbing, Stephanie nodded her head.

Stephanie's paper had originally been done on her brother's old computer. The reason I know this is that Stephanie asked me before she turned it in if I minded pink paper. "Why?" I questioned. "Because I'm using my brother's old computer, and I don't know how to change the paper in the printer," she answered. "My brother says he'll show me how when he comes home for Thanksgiving."

Even on pink paper, I figured that Stephanie would have a step up on revising because she had the use of a computer at home. There was much in her paper worth preserving. But just as much needed to be changed. Stephanie's opening paragraph was a wonderful example of this dichotomy: strong images, vivid sense impressions, and the expression of real feeling — along with an incomplete sentence, a tense change, a pronoun without an antecedent, a dangling participle, misspellings, commas where there should not be commas, and no commas where they were needed.

> The flushing of the toilet, the nauseating gargling of the Listerine, the pleasant yet annoying sounds I use to hear. They came from my best friend. He was a skinny and very ill, elderly man. Wearing a loose fitting ribbed tanktop with pokadot boxer shorts, his silver hair glistened like sand on the beach on a hot summer day. That is what hair he had left. That is how I best remember him. I would watch him scuffle in to his bedroom, careful not to wake anyone still sleeping. After a few minutes, he would reappear this time wearing the same old checkered wool brown pants, and the polyester butterfly collared brown shirt with the horizontal stripes going the wrong way. It never matched.

I made twenty or so comments on Stephanie's paper, concluding with this general one: "This has real potential — and so much love. Your big problem is overwriting, trying too hard to be poetic. Your grandfather himself, if described well, is material enough. Language should make us see him more clearly, not obscure him."

Stephanie didn't conference with me after our initial confrontation over her grade, even though I had invited her to do so. In a way, I sensed that she had too much pride. It was important to her to revise her paper alone, to prove to me — and herself — that she could successfully translate what was in her head to paper. Clearly, the seventeen-year-old Stephanie was more mature than that fifteen year old who thought she could not do anything right no matter how hard she tried.

Working completely from my comments, Stephanie made her changes, combining sentences and generally making her paper more readable. She also improved on the overly poetic language that had obscured her portrait of her grandfather. After I commented on how improved her paper was, Stephanie revealed, "I went through three revisions, read my paper aloud to everyone who would listen, and stayed up until midnight the night before I handed it in."

As a fifteen year old, Stephanie had found it necessary to inform me she was not the smart one. Two years later, she displayed her insecurity and lack of confidence in other ways. Stephanie's concern about her physical appearance became apparent in a short story she wrote toward the end of senior year. In it, she changed into a china ballerina doll.

"Gooooood morning New York, I am David, David Haynes on WPLJ, Power 95 with your burnt toast and coffee time" — a typical morning, until I started to get ready to brush my hair. But I couldn't get the brush through it. I took my eyes off the brush and looked in the mirror as my morning ritual when, I saw I had this weird gold and diamond tiara in my hair. I bet this would have made Elizabeth Taylor jealous. Every strand of my hair was in place. It was parted in the middle, and the length of it was on top of my head in a bun. "How fucking quaint!" I thought. I figured I'd try to get off my bed, walk to the mirror, and get a better close-up view. But I fell flat on the floor onto my butt. I looked down, and my usual size fourteen body was more like a size three, weightwise. My bust had decreased from a 36C to a micro-nothing. My fat thighs were now all muscle including my calves and ankles. You could even count the different muscles in them. I had on a pink body-suit with gold around the small cleavage area I now possessed. The body-suit came up around the top of the bodice, hugging it to every strand of thread on the skimpy outfit. The tutu was more like a one-one due to the thinness of my new shape.

This passage from Stephanie's final version is quite different from the draft she originally handed me. In Stephanie's draft, the action of the story was not clear: the china ballerina doll and the teenager, according to Stephanie's writing, both looked alike. Similarly slim and elegant, the description of the two made it difficult for me to follow the transformation.

Replying to Stephanie in terms of what she had written on the page, I expressed my confusion by saying, "It's not clear to me how you changed. What size were you to begin with? I guess the bigger question is that I'm not sure what you're trying to get across with your description of your appearance. You don't make it sound so bad in the first place." In order to clear up my confusion as a reader, Stephanie made significant changes between this draft and her final revision.

In the section from the revision I quoted earlier, Stephanie let it all hang out: "My usual size fourteen body was more like a size three, weightwise. My bust decreased from a 36C to a micro-nothing. My fat thighs...." More important, though, was that by using fiction as a vehicle, Stephanie began to see herself as she really was, an overweight seventeen year old with large blue eyes and golden brown hair. What's more, she ended up liking what she saw. Stephanie's progress on her short story could have been her first step toward self-acceptance. A second passage from the final version illustrates this movement.

My giddy mom barged into my pig-pen palace and said in her Carol Brady voice, "Honey, it's almost twenty to seven, please hurry up." I nodded my head and proceeded to agree with her and said in my Cindy Brady voice, "Okay, mom, I'll be downstairs when I am ready. Oh, would you please make me some yummy pancakes, especially the kind with lots of raisins?" Gosh, I hate raisins. Every time I eat them I barf up the corpses. Even the thought of eating them makes the hair on my arms stand up. [But] saying I like raisins helps me to score points on mom's good side. I guess that makes me an unperfect, phony person. I often feel like a goody-goody, but I know deep down inside I am not. I get tired of being a role-model daughter, and especially to be letter perfect like my mom. She always matches her perfect fitting clothes. I really could have a wild side being me, like partying without morals, staying out late and admitting I hate raisins.

Stephanie really wanted to be herself: not a "role-model daughter," not her "smart" brother—and especially, not a china ballerina doll. Before this, she had found it difficult to discuss her appearance. But describing herself in the guise of fiction freed Stephanie. When she handed in her final revision, Stephanie was elated: "I'm excited about this paper, because it's *me* talking," she said as she placed it, carefully, on my desk.

As the year progressed, Stephanie worked even harder. Her determination was fueled by her newly achieved self-confidence. The opening of Stephanie's analysis of Hitchcock's film *Psycho* is an example of this new strength.

In Alfred Hitchcock's powerful film, "Psycho," Anthony Perkins portrays Norman Bates, a motel owner who is obsessed with birds. Not only is he preoccupied with these creatures, but he also resembles them. The movie takes place at the Bates Motel, a seedy lodge off the beaten path. Throughout the office of the motel are numerous stuffed birds, authoritative and powerful. Their feathers are expansive and their eyes piercing, as they look down at the viewer. Some are in a swooping position, with their wings spread wide and their mouths open, as though awaiting a victim. They are predators, similar to Norman.

The Bates house is situated high upon a hill, above the motel. The color of the house appears to be muddy. There are dark spots throughout the surface of it, similar to the texture of a bird's body. The residence resembles a bird-house with its copious windows. As the top of the house gets narrower, the windows get smaller. Near the highest point is a large opening with bars that can be compared to a birdcage. The doorway of the house is rounded, a perfect shape for a bird to pop in and out. This is where Norman lives.

In her film analysis Stephanie goes on to show that Norman Bates has the characteristics of a predatory bird and that Marilyn Crane, his birdlike victim, is his unfortunate prey. Although this conclusion may seem obvious, we had not discussed Hitchcock's film in class. Stephanie interpreted it on her own. I was most impressed, though, with her descriptions. She demonstrated to me that she was able to transfer skills she had acquired while writing narrative and fiction to an expository form.

On Stephanie's title page, I scrawled the following comment:

> I really appreciate how hard you work and how doggedly you pursue your own original and creative ideas, rather than taking an easier way out. If you continue to grow in the next three years as much as you have in the three we've known each other, I won't be able to recognize you!

How ironic it was that less than a year later, I didn't recognize Stephanie in the hall!

From the start, Stephanie had exhibited intuitive thinking, a skill that cannot be taught. But it was not until she began to feel confident about her intellectual ability that she had the determination to put her talents and ideas on paper. As a senior, Stephanie proved what I had wanted to—but could not—believe all along: If you don't dwell on technical errors, they will be corrected by the writer when they become important to her.

In her own evaluation at the end of her senior year, Stephanie wrote about her progress:

> The most valuable tool I learned to use this year was to be me. I am a self-assured individual who will live up to my own goals. I enjoyed your comments on my papers, even the negative ones. These were new ideas to expand on, useful in revisions and just in general. I now can write a paper with my own style—that's something no one can take away. I guess all my hours of sitting in front of the computer have really paid off.

The young woman rushing toward me in the hall with a smile on her face had turned out to be a confident person who would be able to achieve her goals.

Paula

Seeking a Role Model

I flung the hairbrush down onto the top of the dresser, and dashed into the bathroom. My hands tore open the shower curtain so forcefully, that three rungs snapped off the curtain rod. My body went into shock from what I saw. There, lying face up on the mat in the tub, was my sister Sue. Her body trembled as the trickling water from the shower nozzle fell on her. Her stiff arms and legs thrashed into the sides of the bathtub while her head jerked to and fro. The paleness of her drawn face was sickening. Her eyes twitched and her nose ran, while saliva slowly slipped out of her half opened mouth.

"Oh, my God," I spoke in silent terror.

"Sue, answer me!" I shouted desperately.

"Mom, help me!" I screamed as I sat inside the tub with my arms wrapped around my sister. My heart beat rapidly, and my eyes filled with tears as I tried to support her vibrating body. Thinking that she might die made my mind go bizurk. I started blurting out feelings that I had been too afraid to say before. "I love you, Sue," I cried. "I'd be lost without you."

This was how Paula described her sister Sue's grand mal seizure in a senior year essay. Instead of dwelling on her pain, though, Paula focused on the positive effects.

My mom, dad, sister, and I, were told by doctors, that in order to be able to deal with Sue's disorder, we would have to start discussing our feelings about it together. It was rough when we first began opening up to each other, but we did share the fact that we all love each other. Hearing everyone express their love was the most wonderful feeling in the world.

I know my family and I will never get used to seeing my sister have a seizure. It is extremely difficult to have to stand by while someone dear is going through pain; knowing there is nothing we can do to prevent it. My family and I just make sure that when we suffer, we suffer together. Although we share a lot of sad feelings now, by learning how to share bad feelings, we have also learned how to share good ones. We all communicate better than I ever dreamed we could.

Very few seventeen year olds would have been able to express such an experience in positive terms. From the start, Paula seemed different, more mature than her classmates. I regularly saw her during first period, from 7:40 to 8:25. Paula would tumble into class, t-shirt hanging out over her sweats, long, tawny hair stuffed into a baseball cap, wide green eyes half open. Relaxing her athletic body in a wooden chair, Paula would stuff something into her mouth. "Breakfast," she explained.

Unlike many of her classmates, Paula not only looked as though she were comfortable with herself, she actually was. Paula wrote in her journal:

> Pertaining to my life, I don't think I see life as a game. I'm not trying to fool myself or anyone else. I'm pretty straightforward. If I have a goal, I will do what I must do and want to achieve it. For instance, I'm awaiting a college interview for art. Since I was a freshman, I've been creating pieces of work that would make up a good portfolio. This wasn't a game to me. I liked what I was doing. Now I'm in the most advanced art class, Portfolio 2, and feel I'm prepared to take college art courses. I keep striving for my goal to receive a Masters in Fine Arts. I know if I want to achieve my goal, I must take many art classes, but if that's what I want, then I don't think it's a game.
>
> ... Some of my friends' parents have pushed them in the directions they are headed. I can tell that they really don't want what their parents want, but are afraid to go against their parents. They go to their classes and get straight A's, but they don't really care. ...

Paula knew why she was going to college and what she wanted to achieve; her goals were her own.

It wasn't until the year was almost half over, though, that I realized how many talents she had. Not only was she an athlete and an artist, but she was also a musician. I discovered this when Paula responded to one of my assignments by writing an original song. She performed it in front of the class, accompanied by a recording of her own piano music. Even with these gifts, though, Paula remained humble, relaxed, and friendly in her quiet way.

She was also a good English student. Not overly bright, complicated, or skillful with language, Paula was not the top student in the class. Nevertheless, she took suggestions and worked hard. She was independent, open, and able to express her thoughts and feelings. What's more, she cared about her work and responded to criticism, improving throughout the year. At times, I wonder if I should have chosen someone else for these stories; she was almost too easy to observe.

Since Paula did well from the start, I didn't take time to look at her writing folder from previous years until January. When I opened it, I read comments like "This still needs work, Paula. It is unfocused and often too general. There are also places where your facts are incorrect or your ideas are unsupported." I also saw the mediocre grades that Paula's carelessly written work had earned.

What's going on, I wondered? She's never turned in anything to me that hasn't been carefully typed. Paula seemed to work harder for me than she had in previous English classes. I didn't know why, but in her year-end evaluation, Paula wrote:

> The way you let me go off in my own direction in choosing a thesis on a paper definitely helped me. Instead of being assigned one or two topics and being forced to choose, I was able to write about what interested me. I liked that. Your editing process and encouragement to revise also helped me to become a better writer.

Able to choose her own topics, to pursue her ideas, and to profit from criticism, Paula seemed to like my class. She was somehow motivated to work hard. Paula responded to, and flourished in, the same conditions that confused Jennifer and others whom I have taught. For me, Paula seemed the perfect student.

One of Paula's first pieces of writing senior year, "Let the Good Times Roll," had been about one of her favorite places in fourth grade, the roller rink. In her conclusion, she highlighted her personal philosophy.

> Everything was so simple then. We were all friends who didn't even know what the word "clique" meant. Nobody judged anybody else. The best part about being in the fourth grade was that you could be yourself. Now that we are all older, a lot of the people that I was once friends with, have changed. They wouldn't even consider going to the roller rink now, because they are afraid of what others might think or say. . . .

Although Paula recreated what it had been like to be nine years old, one of the problems with that paper was lack of specificity. I commented: "Can you describe individuals in the group?" "Was this just girls — or boys, too?" "Can you remember any of the songs?" The following paragraph from Paula's revision illustrates how well she responded to these questions.

> I don't know what it was, but even the sweetest of all the girls and the shyest of all boys became hell on wheels when they began to roll. Around and around we went, whizzing by all the adults and little kids. Once in awhile a skate guard would tell us to slow down. We would go slowly for about five minutes, and then we'd pick up the pace again. We were the fleetest things on that floor. The wind whipped through our hair as we smiled and clapped our hands to the beat of the loud music that was being played by the disc jockey. The song "Love is a Battlefield" by Pat Benetar really got us excited. When we heard this lively tune with its catchy rhythm, we moved our feet even faster.

I couldn't help but laugh when I read this, wondering how I had forgotten Pat Benetar! But Paula's writing brought back even more memories — of myself in fourth grade as I walked over Dorset Avenue Bridge to the Ventnor Heights Roller Rink with my skates hanging over my shoulder.

Paula continued to advance steadily. In March she took a quantum leap, stunning me with the originality of her insights. When we finished reading *A Streetcar Named Desire*, she asked if she could do her paper on alcoholism. I was surprised because I hadn't emphasized alcoholism while teaching the play, so I replied, "Be careful. Don't simplify the play or the characters." Paula came into class the next day, her eyes sparkling. "I've done some research, Mrs. Lott. It all fits perfectly."

In her paper, Paula argued that the four phases of response to alcoholism were present in Tennessee Williams's play. Even her ploy to get the reader to accept this idea was cleverly handled in her introductory paragraph.

> Living with an alcoholic is a family affair. Because it subjects all members of a household to constant stress and fears of various kinds, it has often been referred to as a "family illness." To one degree or another all members of the family are influenced. Throughout the play, "A Streetcar Named Desire," by Tennessee Williams, the four phases of responses to alcoholism are followed. Williams created a family that went through each stage of responses to alcoholism without defining each stage. Therefore, because the theme of alcoholism is written between the lines, the reader must either choose to look deeper into the possibility of alcoholism, or choose to deny that alcohol is present, just as alcoholics do.

Paula not only supported her thesis well, but she also explained the ramifications of alcoholism clearly. Here are her remarks on the first phase of alcoholism:

> The first phase of responses to alcoholism is called the reactive phase. During this time, most family members become extremely cautious in their behavior in order to avoid or to further complicate the existing problems of alcoholism. However, by being reactive they are constantly adapting their behavior in order to minimize or survive an unhealthy situation. Much of this adaption will not only have detrimental effects on those adjusting, but also it indirectly allows and supports the continuing alcoholism.

When Blanche arrived at Stanley and Stella's house in New Orleans, one of the first things she did was secretly guzzle down a half tumbler of whiskey before she even saw her sister. Then when she did see her sister, she said, "Open your pretty mouth and talk while I look for some liquor." Soon after that, Blanche said, "Now don't get worried, your sister hasn't turned into a drunkard." Stella just sat back and watched Blanche parade around the apartment. She didn't do anything to stop Blanche's absurd behavior. It was apparent, also, that Blanche was showing signs of denial by telling her sister she wasn't an alcoholic.

Denial is a main characteristic of the reactive phase. It is ironic that family members deny a drinking problem in their families, because that is exactly what the alcoholic does. For an alcoholic, like Blanche, denial is functional for the continuation of drinking. As long as the alcoholic denies that she has a drinking problem, there is no reason to seek a solution. Non alcoholic family members, such as Stella, also deny, but their denial is totally dysfunctional to meeting their needs. Everyone in the family denies that anything is wrong, yet nobody feels right.

After I read Paula's initial paper, I asked her if she knew that Tennessee Williams himself was an alcoholic. She didn't, but this information led her to conclude her revised essay this way:

> Tennessee Williams did not write that alcoholism was involved in his play, but he inferred it. He may not have even done it purposely, because from what I understand, Williams himself was an alcoholic. Only due to research was I able to see how much alcohol had an effect on how each character acted. It was surprising to find that the characters went through each stage of responses to alcoholism. It is much easier to understand a certain behavior when you know what causes it.
>
> Because alcoholism isn't stressed in Tennessee Williams words, and can only be inferred, he is giving the reader the choice to look deeper into the possibility of alcoholism, or the choice to deny it. If only people would stop denying and start trying, this world would be a much more sober place.

Although Paula's final line was somewhat polemical for my taste, I could not help but be impressed with her insights and arguments. Early in the year, I had seen Paula as receptive and hard working. Now I was beginning to see her as an insightful reader, capable of original papers.

Paula's abilities grew throughout the year. Yet she remained that same cooperative person who had walked into class in September. When I assigned group work to compare two Wordsworth sonnets, Paula took charge of her group. Due to absences and recalcitrant members, she stayed up until four in the morning the day their paper was due. I did not know any of this until I read her self-evaluation.

Why didn't Paula complain? Why didn't she ask to meet with me and request an extension? She probably should have. I didn't understand her behavior, though, until I read her course evaluation at the end of the year. Paula makes an implicit statement about herself and her need for a role model that is possibly true for others her age as well:

> The most enjoyable part of this course was getting to know you. In most of my other courses, my teachers treat their students as though they are numbers. The main reason that I looked forward to English class, was because you put yourself on the same level as us and established comfortable relationships with each of us by sharing your personal experiences. Even if you just said something about what you and your husband did on your anniversary, or shared a story that your husband wrote, that really meant a lot. I have, and I'm sure many other people have a great deal of respect for you. I can tell that you've gone through some pretty rough times, but because you chose to move on with your life, you've accomplished great things. . . .
>
> You see, you must realize, because I am only seventeen, I look up to you. I see how successful your life is, and can only pray that mine will be as good. I can't even imagine what I'm going to be in the future. I am at a very impressionable age, and you've made a greater impact on my life than you'll ever know. It is because of teachers like yourself that make students want to continue studying a certain subject. I'm looking forward to taking writing courses in college. . . .

Throughout the year, I had had no idea that Paula was particularly drawn to me. She responded positively to my teaching, but never hung around my desk or dropped by the English office or in any way let me know that I was particularly important to her. She did her work—period. Before I read her evaluation, I hadn't known that she needed a role model. For whatever reason, Paula and I met at a time in her life when I was important to her. Before senior year, Paula's interests in school had been art, music, and athletics. Now, she was "looking forward to taking writing courses in college."

As teachers, it is hard to be sure who we influence or how we influence them. Very often our effect can be more powerful and lasting than we imagine. Paula ended her evaluation this way: "Thank you for keeping my doors open to a future that will definitely include writing."

Reflections

*L*ast April, Paul Clark and I registered for a conference sponsored by The Northern New Jersey Writing Con-
sortium called "Perspectives on Student Writing." We
attended workshops on journal writing, portfolios, and multicultural education. The greatest change of perspective for me
occurred, however, each time I glanced at my colleague.

Paul, a big, bearded man, wore jeans. Surrounded by hundreds of neatly dressed women in tailored suits, I could not
help but be struck by his counterculture maleness. It seemed
as though the majority of writing teachers — or at least those
who attended conferences in northern New Jersey — were
women. Lil Brannon, a keynote speaker, also remarked on
this, in political terms. "It is men who tell mothers what to
do," she said, discussing her image of the educational hierar-
chy and the writing classroom. In our department, Paul is one
of two males among eleven females. And, judging from the
percentage of men who have recently applied for job open-
ings, this ratio is not unusual.

In terms of my own teaching experience, of the students I
studied over the course of the year, I felt as though I worked
as effectively as I would have liked with four. Of these four,
three were women. My reflections are hardly a scientific analysis, and the original group was not equally divided by gender
but, nevertheless, I have to confess I related more easily to
other women. Perhaps this is because we shared similar experiences. Interested in the humanities before they entered my
classroom, Jane, Stephanie, and Paula were also interested in
me as a person and in what I had to teach.

Gender issues, though, occur in a larger field than the classroom. Women in our society may very well share a common

culture. Deborah Tannen writes in her bestseller *You Just Don't Understand* (1990) that women speak the same language. Generally, more than men, women like to talk things out. Concerned with the complexities of experience, we are often less practiced than men at simplifying, at concentrating on segments rather than entireties.

Jane and I enjoyed talking things out in our informal conferences. And I was pleased that Jane learned how to include complexities in an organized piece of writing. As it turned out, Stephanie, too, achieved the most when she was able to look at the complexities of her situation. She grew as a writer at the same time that she became comfortable with her physical appearance and her assessment of herself.

Furthermore, in a world where cultural expectations for women are constantly shifting, we look to each other for role models. Paula did this, just as I do when I meet women whom I admire.

Of course, none of us is completely defined by gender. Culturally, we are influenced in many ways. I value writing as part of life. When Paula wrote that her "future . . . will definitely include writing," I felt successful as her teacher. Since my overall goal was to involve my students in being writers and not merely have them learn writing recipes, I was impressed with Jane's, Stephanie's, and Paula's achievements.

Elizabeth, a colleague of mine in the English department, might have thought otherwise. She values the perfect paragraph. Wind Elizabeth up and she'll tell you. She doesn't understand how students can write compositions if they can't write paragraphs. Patient and effective, Elizabeth is a good teacher. Her students and colleagues know this. Paragraph by paragraph, her classes draft, meet in writing groups, and revise. Yet Elizabeth and I see the teaching of writing differently.

And so do English teachers across the country. In the March 1991, issue of *English Journal*, Ben Nelms submitted my story, "Jeremy: Sex, Lies, and Masks," to the scrutiny of five peers who are national leaders in English education. Although their pedagogical values and mine are all very close, their responses all differed. Bill Lyons pointed out that my assigned topic almost asked "for phoney language"; Ted Hipple cheered my efforts at getting Jeremy to write. Dixie Dellinger wrote about a student of hers; Denise Standiford brought up feminist issues; George Shea mentioned audience, purpose, style, and sentence structure. We all approach the teaching of writing from our own angles, just as each of these stories will be viewed in different ways.

What then was personally satisfying to me about these three previous stories? To begin with, none of the interactions were one sided. Unlike my manipulation of Jennifer to rewrite "Black Hats and Ribbons," or Joseph's manipulation of me to allow him to remain at his computer, movement took place on both sides of the desk. If I had not been open to Jane's conference style, she might have remained closeted. If I had not been comfortable with Stephanie and Paula pursuing their own ideas, they might not have progressed. I grew along with my students.

Moreover, growth for my students was personal as well as academic. Stephanie moved from thinking her brother was "the smart one" in the family to feeling confident about her own abilities. Jane moved from needing lengthy conferences to working independently. Looking at Stephanie's papers, I could see that she transferred skills she had developed in writing narration and fiction to expository forms. Paula demonstrated that she could hypothesize and support an original analysis of a well-known writer's play. I was lucky enough to have seen these students at a point when their maturation seemed evident.

This is rarely possible. Usually, I am confined to teaching a series of fifty-minute periods over the course of a single year. Often, I learn nothing about my students after school closes in June. This can make teaching a fragmenting and lonely experience. In contrast, over a three-year period I saw Stephanie transform from a sophomore who wasn't sure her thoughts were worthwhile, to a senior who had enough assurance to say, "I'm excited about this paper, because it's *me* talking."

Rarely can high school teachers—because of large classes, teaching loads, tight schedules, and bureaucratic structures—establish a continuous relationship with students. Sadly, we often miss out on the excitement of seeing the results of our teaching.

As a mother, I know firsthand that it sometimes takes years to see children develop. My middle daughter, Suzanne, wrote notes to her friends in the back rows of her high school English classes, never opting for the honors track. And although Suzanne's ability was not a concern to me, she only got okay grades in high school. Not until she attended Hampshire College did she become interested in literature and in her own writing. She graduated from Hampshire in three years, writing a novel as her senior thesis. Suzanne is now teaching at a university English department and publishing short stories of her own.

Suzanne's college experiences encouraged her to become a creative thinker. Although my daughter ultimately chose writing as a career, creative thinking is important in any field. Kimon Nicolaides, an art teacher, suggests:

> The job of the teacher, as I see it, is to teach students, not how to draw but how to learn to draw. They must acquire some real method of finding out facts for themselves lest they be limited for the rest of their lives to facts the instructor relates. They must discover something of the true nature of artistic creation—of the hidden processes by which inspiration works.

I was fortunate enough to be able to participate in this sort of learning situation with Jane, Stephanie, and Paula. All three of these students took their education into their own hands. My task had been not so much to *teach* them as to encourage *learning*.

Part Four

Struggling for Perspective

Each case is a slice of someone's life. The lessons it suggests will vary for each reader. To put it differently, each case is a kaleidoscope: what you see in it depends on how you shake it.

— Abby J. Hansen, *Teaching and the Case Method*

Jeremy

Sex, Lies, and Masks

I taught Jeremy four years prior to teaching the other students whose stories are in this book. Then a relatively new teacher, I had not yet written about my work, nor had I had much opportunity to reflect upon it. Nevertheless, Jeremy's story remained vivid in my mind. Although from time to time I forget the lessons that Jeremy taught me, I never forget how valuable those lessons were.

Jeremy was a sophomore in my Honors English II class, even though he really wasn't supposed to be there. My department head informed me on the first day of school that Jeremy had not earned a high enough score on the eighth grade writing sample to enter Honors English I, nor had his English I teacher recommended him for Honors English II, and a teacher's recommendation is necessary to enter an honors-level course after freshman year. Jeremy had pushed his way into the class. He had complained about his previous teacher and his course of study to the principal, and his parents had reinforced his complaints with theirs. So there Jeremy was, in my class, a good-looking, overgrown, insecure, rebellious fifteen year old, whose defense was that he was superior to everyone else in the room, including me.

To tell the truth, though, I rather liked him. His rebellious attitude was kind of refreshing in a room full of grade-grubbing honors students, and his negative remarks stimulated our discussions. My initial impression was that Jeremy was capable of being in Honors; that is, until he submitted his first paper, "What Is Important to Me."

The topic was of the same genre as "What I Did over My Summer Vacation," and was assigned with the objective of getting to know the students and getting a feel for how they wrote. The month before, I had attended Northeastern University's Summer Institute at Martha's Vineyard and had written an essay, entitled "Island Memory." In it, I discussed growing up on an island and later feeling trapped. Reading this aloud to the class before they began their own writing process, I encouraged them to be honest about what was important to them. Here are Jeremy's first three paragraphs:

Sex ... What? Yes, S-E-X, that obnoxious three-letter word that is supposedly oblivious to one's cerebrum. As I have found, everything of importance in life is the edifice for the foundation of sex; or for the humans offspring's sexual purposes. Halt!! Before I go into any more detail, I would like to declare that if you, the reader are offended, disturbed, perturbed or disordered heretofore, the continual reading of this rhetoric should be terminated at this point and no further.

Primarily, the minute the metomorphic transition from embryo to fetus transpires, the fetuses main aspiring endeaver in life is successfully transacting in pleasurable sexual encounters (in the unconscious). The life bearing parentage's aspirations are double sought: 1) synonomous with child 2) capricious desire for child to have unlimited and unrestricted access to all females he might contemplate.

However, few, my "importances" pertain to the latter, for the initial inkling would be far too tedious and encumbersome at this point in time. When my, perchance; son (not to be sexist) is acquired with the state of existence or birth, I will then, begin my teachings or shall I say preachings on everything and most of all "nothing." Do not perceive me incorrectly, I am not literally, verbally articulating with him, more so, be a gesticulateing, communicative process, enabling us to formulate a type of liason.

It took me quite a while to read Jeremy's paper: the first time through my eyes bulged; the second time I found myself muttering, "What the hell is he trying to say?" Finally, on the third reading, I began to laugh.

It took me even longer to decide on a grade. Jeremy was smart, too smart for his own good; he had already covered himself. Certainly, he would accuse me of being an "offended" reader if I failed him. My final decision was not to grade Jeremy's paper at all. Instead, I wrote the following comment: "Why did you find it necessary to write in such a phoney voice? It doesn't work; it only obscures what you are trying to say. If these ideas are important to you, revise your paper, but have the guts to write your thoughts straight out."

Jeremy looked down his nose from the back of the room as he half listened to the various refrains of, "What Is Important to Me" that were read aloud as examples of good writing. They might be the teacher's idea of good writing, but I could see from the expression on Jeremy's face that they certainly were not his! When the students finished commenting on the papers that were read, I walked around the room and returned the rest of the essays, telling the students to read over their comments and to arrange for a conference if they had questions. After Jeremy looked at his paper, he stretched his long legs out into the aisle and scowled down at his desk. He never raised his eyes to look at me.

Although I must admit I did worry a little about my approach, a week later, when Jeremy handed in his revision, I patted myself on the back. That was before I read it. Unfortunately, it was not much better than his first paper had been. If anything, it was even more pompous. His first paragraph follows:

> "What is important to me" is the subject given for me to write about for my personal essay. Although I feel my previous rough copy was a masterpiece, my teacher disagrees and therefore I am compelled to sit at my table and reconstruct a refined paper considering the fact that in this society that I live in constitutes my teacher the right to give her opinion in a form of a permenant grade. I must abide.

The rest of the paper continues with little change.

I read Jeremy's revision and wondered if it would ever be possible to teach him anything. To Jeremy, school was a game that pitted him against the teacher. Learning was irrelevant to him, or so it appeared.

How different was Jeremy from his classmates? The biggest difference I could see was that I could teach them. School was a game to most of them as well, but they won by trying to please me. "How many pages do you want, Mrs. Lott?" "Do you want a long introduction?" "Are two examples enough?" How often had I said, "It's your paper. I can only give you suggestions. You must think for yourself"? Apparently, Jeremy didn't even want suggestions.

Jeremy played games with language, too, covering up his own voice with one he couldn't yet manage. I remembered playing the younger version of this years ago — "dress-ups" — shuffling around in my mother's high-heeled shoes.

Speaking of shoes, at the bottom of Jeremy's paper, he wrote, "Mrs. Lott, if I projected myself into your shoes and tried to grade a paper I was morally against, I would have incredible difficulty with this (probably an almost impossible task), but I ask you to try to grade this paper in an unbiased way."

As far as I was aware, Jeremy knew nothing about me or my morals. It was all too ridiculous. At my wit's end, I gave him the F he deserved. His language was awkward and wordy, and his paper was impossible to understand. I underlined *masterpiece*, writing "My dictionary defines this as 'a great work of art.' Come on now, Jeremy." I then underlined *refined*, and wrote "Your first paper was 'refined.' That wasn't the problem." After attacking Jeremy up and down the margins of his revised essay, I made my final "un-teacherly" comment: "This is a bunch of gibberish. I'm seriously beginning to doubt whether you are capable of clearly stating your ideas within a paper. Your total lack of humility is standing like a stone barrier and blocking you from learning. If you are not willing to stop hiding behind it, if you don't have the guts to tear it down, you'll never learn anything."

When he received his grade and comments, Jeremy glared at me from the back of the room, sulked for two days without contributing one word to class discussions, and then, on the third day, asked to have a conference with me after school. I wish I could remember everything we said at that conference. Mostly I remember how I felt, though I do recall that Jeremy walked in acting superior as usual and began to talk to me as though I was a weak-minded, pathetic female. At that point, I closed the door, so that we could have a real shouting match.

I yelled that if he wasn't able to accept comments on his writing, he wouldn't remain in Honors English II, and he shouted his accusations back at me. This went on for at least five minutes, but after we got that business out of the way, we began to talk. I told Jeremy that as far as I was concerned he could write anything he wanted; sex didn't bother me. Jeremy recreated our dialogue in his journal this way:

> I received the conference I requested with Mrs. Lott. I was honest with her and she was honest with me. At first I could tell she felt insecure because she tended to purposely put me on the spot like a sadist but after five minutes, we really started talking about me, her, my paper and class. . . . Well, I feel Mrs. Lott and I really got much accomplished through our discussion. Most of all I feel she better understands me and that is advantageous for both of us.

Jeremy remained somewhat defensive and egotistical. Not surprisingly, though, the second line of Jeremy's journal entry was "I was honest with her and she was honest with me." Playing the role of teacher and student, with all the underlying insecurities that these roles mask, doesn't make for the most honest of relationships. Jeremy knew that. But was Jeremy also beginning to realize that honesty might be an issue in his writing as well? A week later, Jeremy handed me his final revision. The first two pages follow:

> In awe, I covertly pasted my eyes on their voluptuous bodies. Unaware of my scrutiny, they proceeded to babble to them-

selves, probably concerning some football scoring machine or else, no doubt, a California surfing stud with a beautifully built bronzed bod. On numerous occasions I had tried to avert their attention to me, but always to no avail.

Teasing myself, visually probing every curve of their torsos, I . . .

"Okay," the teacher said brusquely, I, snapping out of my usual dose of morning lust.

"Settle down. For the last week, your assignment has been to write a rough draft on the topic 'What is Important to Me'. Please group together in threes or fours and read your papers to each other; then comment constructively on each paper. . . ."

The young ladies glanced toward me and provacatively gestured for me to obediently join them. I was so awestruck by the idea of them wanting me in their clan that I was speechless. After five or ten seconds of panic and dither, I courageously managed to raise my hand and motion for *them* to join *me* at my present location, the secluded desk in the corner of the room. (Thinking back, I don't know how I came up with the audacity.)

The two politely agreed and sleekly made their way over to my table. I, of course, taking full advantage of the situation, eyeballed every bit of exposed flesh on their hourglass-shaped bodies.

"Hi," they said practically in unison.

"How's it hangin'?" I cooly replied and then found myself taking over.

"I didn't get a chance to write a rough draft, but I have all of my ideas safelocked up here (pointing to my head), so why don't you both read and if there is time I'll talk a litle bit about the inspirational thoughts I have for my future paper."

Surely enough, they concurred and I had an incredibly encumbering task: it was to listen attentively to two of the most pathetically drab essays I have ever heard.

Upon the completion of the essays, I gazed over towards my teacher in a leering manner. Unfortunately, she was preoccupied and wasn't about to tell the class to stop. The gorgeous girls complained impatiently that I should speak about the paper I was going to write.

"I must satisfy these babes!" I thought, feeling coerced into revealing my innermost self.

"Okay, . . . well you see," I stammered, feeling as though they were about to be stupefied. "The only thing that is important that I could think of is sex." I then watched as their jaws dropped. "You see," I said, "I've noticed that almost any voluntary action I make is for one stimulus, sex." I could tell the latter statement blew their minds because their cute prima donna faces transfigured into a deep cherry flush and then they fidgeted uncontrollably in their seats. "And to write about another subject would be utterly untrue to myself and others who read the paper." Then I added what seemed to be a spark dropped in a keg of gunpowder. "I also feel that almost everybody I know, including yourselves, do everything for sexual pleasure."

Jeremy's subject remained the same—sex was what was important to him—but instead of using language to obscure the importance of sex, he told the truth, his truth, a fifteen-year-old male's truth—"snapping out of my usual dose of morning lust." Because Jeremy told the truth, his essay was straightforward and clear. There was no wordiness, no obscure language, no redundancies, and no generalities. What's more, it was fun to read.

From the start, Jeremy was willing to risk saying that sex was what was important to him, but it took some mudslinging before he was willing to risk writing about sex clearly. Jeremy's outrageous choice of subject matter on the one hand and the way he used language to obfuscate on the other— combined with his defensive attitude toward me— aggravated me to such an extent that I finally did what teachers aren't supposed to do: I blew my cool. (I wish, as a more experienced teacher, I had exhibited the same lack of restraint with Bill, the protagonist of my next story, a few years later.)

Like a thunderstorm on a hot summer day, anger cleared the air between us. Because I dropped my teacher's mask of superiority, Jeremy was willing to drop his. We began to listen to each other. After that, Jeremy began to learn. And he didn't have any further problems in Honors English II.

Over the next two years, whenever I happened to see Jeremy in the hall, I couldn't help but notice that his visible identity appeared to be in a continuous state of flux. By the time senior year arrived, he was no longer wearing t-shirts hanging out over his jeans as he had as a sophomore. Instead, he dressed like an advertisement for Brooks Brothers in button-down shirts, ties, and jackets. "They're my father's," he told me when I remarked on his attire.

Whenever we stopped to chat, I would ask Jeremy about the progress he was making in his classes. According to him, he was doing well. Continuing on the honors track, he selected AP English senior year.

His personality, however, remained the same. One of his friends told me that when Jeremy entered college he changed his last name. And, when I asked his permission to reprint his work, I received this letter:

> I'm not certain if the *English Journal* article will be reprinted or if you have reworked your piece—but I took the liberty of counting the number of words in the article.
>
> My words, and words appearing in my journal; account for: 1134 words (approx)—(1015 are actually my own words). The remaining # of words (all yours) totals: (approx) 1103 words.
>
> Given the fact that the ratio is about 1:1 I have only 2 Requests: 1) That, aside from any "big bucks" you gross, I would like a copy of the book sent/given to me.
>
> and:
>
> 2) That I may use (though I probably won't) these publications as references on my resume as having my work published. (a note of recognition in a "preamble" of some sort wouldn't hurt either!)

Finishing his letter on a warm note, Jeremy wished me luck, offered me help "publicizing" my book, and suggested we get in touch. Similar to my reaction four years before when Jeremy was in my sophomore class, I read what he had written, my eyes bulged, I found myself muttering, and, finally, I began to laugh.

Bill

Resisting Control

Each time I have begun to write one of these stories, my mood has been one of expectation, similar to the excitement I feel before seeing someone I have not been with in over a year. Often, I have sat in front of my computer cursing or smiling, even laughing out loud. I have murmured to myself "I haven't thought of that in a long time"; "I wish I hadn't done that"; or "I really miss that kid." I didn't feel that way about Bill.

It wasn't that Bill was a poor student—his grades were good. Even while he challenged my control and resisted my comments, his writing progressed. In fact, upon reflection I realized that his poetry, which I had criticized, had affected his prose in a positive manner. Nor could I help admiring his individuality. Left to his own devices, Bill was often creative and insightful. At the time, however, I didn't see him that way. I am almost ashamed to admit this, but I ignored Bill.

When I realized that he would continue to reject my influence, I stopped caring. After all, I did have over a hundred other students, some of whom let me know they needed me. I never let myself know Bill. Perhaps that is why his story is especially difficult to write.

From the start, Bill had the habits of a good English student. When I checked summer reading lists, his was long. Chatting with me before class, he told me he wrote poetry. In fact, I remembered reading one of his poems in the school literary magazine. When I asked my colleagues in the English department about him, I discovered that until that year Bill had been in Honors English. Choosing not to take AP English, he ended up in my section. I thought that he seemed to have ability and should progress easily, not expecting problems. Oddly enough, the problems I experienced teaching Bill turned out to be another aspect of the qualities I admired.

The difficulties began in October when he asked if his autobiographical writing could be in the form of a poem. After some thought, I hesitantly agreed, satisfied that he was fairly proficient in what I had been reviewing in class. Why not let him choose the form his paper will take? Little did I suspect that Bill's poem would be about a drug dealer.

> *He walks the streets alone*
> *Constantly looking for a new victim —*
> *Young*
> *Old*
> *Black*
> *White*
> *Successful*
> *Poor*
> *It makes no difference to him,*
> *All he cares about is the money.*
>
> *If you're thirsty,*
> *He's got coke;*
> *If that's flat,*
> *He'll give you ice;*
>
> *After your mouth is dry,*
> *He'll give you bazooka.*
> *For the little kids,*
> *He's got stamps.*
> *And for the old, pipes.*
> *It makes no difference to him,*
> *All he cares about is the money.*

Bill's third verse continued in a similar vein, beginning with "His victims suffer" and ending with the two-line refrain of the previous stanzas. It was only in one line, though (the third from the last in this final verse) that Bill shared "his autobiography."

He is the scum of the nation;
Tearing it apart from the inside out.
He has to be stopped.
Now!
For if he isn't,
He will continue his ways;
He will continue to walk the streets.
Walking into your house
My house
The White House
Every house
I am committed to stopping him.
But, it makes no difference to him,
All he cares about is the money.

My first response was to tell Bill that his poem was not autobiographical. Maybe if I had stopped there and immediately insisted that Bill redo the assignment, we would have gotten to know each other. But I avoided butting heads. Instead, I responded to what Bill had written. "I like your flat language and street rhythms," I told him. Then I asked, "What do you know about drugs?"

Amazed that I would ask *him* such a question, Bill answered disdainfully, "I've never even had a sip of alcohol. I don't believe in drugs."

"It's hard to write about what you don't know," I interjected.

Assuming the role of expert always brings out the worst in me and Bill disagreed. "I'm a member of PUSH, an organization that goes into the lower schools to warn students against the use of drugs. I've even attended their national convention. There's nothing I don't know about drugs."

Annoyed, I tried a new approach. "Do you know what *didactic* means?" Bill admitted he didn't. "Well, look it up," I suggested. "Your last verse seems somewhat didactic to me."

Bill came into class early the next day, not to listen but to continue his defense. "I looked up *didactic*. None of my friends think you're right."

"Have you ever tried writing a poem from the druggie's point of view?" I asked. Bill just stared. "Why don't you?" I suggested.

Thus, Bill and I began our antagonistic relationship. Although he craved my admiration for whatever he wrote, he didn't want suggestions about how to improve. On the other hand, I craved his admiration for my teaching skills. And I wanted him to take my suggestions.

When Bill came to me for "help" with his college essay, we repeated this same behavior. Again, he had written about his work with PUSH and how strongly he felt about the evils of drugs. When I suggested that he change some of his rhetoric in order to give a fuller, more personal picture of himself, he cut me off. "My grandmother's a writer," he told me. "She worked with me on this and said it's just fine." Tit for tat, I thought, and cut Bill off as well.

Still, he troubled me. I couldn't figure out what Bill's purpose was in writing. Certainly not to convince or persuade others. Even though I was his teacher, he seemed uninterested in my reaction. Why didn't Bill want to write out of his own experience? Why did he seem unwilling to make discoveries?

I had no answers to these questions until I began to write this story. Finally, almost a year later, it dawned on me: Bill wrote to convince himself, to create an image of himself—an "aura," as he called it in a journal entry.

"Your soul is the whole world." I feel that this quote is fairly correct when it comes to me. I take "soul," in this instance, to mean beliefs and "world" to mean what you perceive yourself as. I will use one example to illustrate how this plays in my life. As you know I am *very very* strongly anti-drug and alcohol. I have never had a joint, cigarette or alcohol, except for Manichevitz on Passover, in my life. No lie. Ask anyone who knows me. Anyway, because of my strong beliefs, my friends and peers have come to know that those are my beliefs and that nothing can change them. I have earned their respect and honor because of these, and I know that if any of my close friends would catch me with a beer or anything in my hand they would take it away and practically kill me. I have created an aura around me that says "no drugs!" That aura is my world.

When a student writes to justify himself or to defend his identity, he is not much interested in feedback from his teacher.

And although I admired Bill's idealism and certainly agreed with him about the horrors of drugs, he angered and frustrated me. One night I mused in my journal:

Bill uses language the way I imagine an artist creating a commissioned portrait uses paints—to flatter. Bill paints himself, though, and he never looks beneath the surface. Would it be an exaggeration to say that Bill's writing is narcissistic? He stares into the pool admiring his own image. But because his image is attractive and his brush strokes nicely done, he gets by. I don't know how to help him progress.

Perhaps I just needed to be patient, I reasoned—to ignore him and not let him get to me. That tack seemed to work for awhile. Both he and I liked the essay he wrote about *The Graduate*. Bill's introduction follows:

Still. That is the first thing I notice about a fish tank. The little plants that are dispersed about the tank are still. The water is still. Even the fish in the tank appear calm and melancholy. Swimming softly through the water without any disruption, they eat, swim, and eat again. There is no excitement in their little home. In the film "The Graduate," directed by Mike Nichols, Benjamin Braddock (Dustin Hoffman) had such a life. It was apparent through his motions and his monotonous tone of voice that he had not experienced much excitement, including his years at college. Much like the fish, he went through the typical motions of life calm, bored, and melancholy. But all that changed as soon as Mrs. Robinson (Ann Bancroft) threw his keys into the tank.

Capturing Nichols's metaphor of the fish tank, Bill played with language in his introduction the way a poet would. When I complimented him, telling him he wrote with style,

Bill was elated. He liked praise. And although he had not previously responded to my comments, which had been in the form of questions and personal reactions, I noticed that he was willing to make necessary revisions on this paper as long as my remarks specifically related to his text. In his revision, Bill put events in order, changed tenses, and corrected a problem he had had distinguishing between a literal and symbolic action. Our deadlock broken, I felt better. But I still couldn't get a handle on him. His "snob act" got in the way. Not only did he behave as though he knew more than I did, but he also gave me the impression that he thought he was better than the rest of the class, an impression verified by Bill's journal.

> Firstly, I would like to address the pathetic discussion that was held in class today. I think that some of the answers to the question, "Do we have to leave our parents to find ourselves?" were okay, but the rationales were pretty shitty, in my opinion. You may wonder why I didn't join the discussion then? Sometimes I just like to sit and listen. I feel that when you leave your parents it doesn't mean a physical get-up-and-go. I feel that it's when you start to see the world in your own eyes, start to believe in what you want, and have your own personal feelings about most subjects, not just what your parents want you to see.
>
> I personally didn't have to leave physically, because I have had my own beliefs about my religion, my people and their past, drugs and alcohol, and most of what has gone on in the world for some time now. I know what I believe in and nothing people say will persuade me.

Inasmuch as I enjoyed Bill's class, I resented the fact that Bill thought we held "pathetic discussions." Why, then, didn't he join in and attempt to improve them? It became more and more apparent that Bill sat and listened from what he deemed to be a position of superiority. As he mentioned in his journal, he knew what he believed in and nothing anyone could say would persuade him otherwise. According to Bill, he had nothing further to learn. To all outward appearances, the "aura" that Bill created around himself not only said "No drugs!" it also said "Socially superior!" Bill polished this aura assiduously. In fact, he was so busy with his aura that he found it difficult to learn.

Unable to teach him, I decided the next time Bill and I met head to head, I would change my tactics. Instead of beating around the bush, I would assert myself strongly. This happened sooner than I wished.

Having studied at The Lincoln Center Institute, a program in which teachers engage with playwrights, directors, dancers, musicians, and artists in aesthetic education, I was instrumental in bringing a production of *A Midsummer Night's Dream* to the high school. A teacher-artist came from Lincoln Center to work with my students and those of another faculty member who was also a participant. Bill's class read the play, acted out their own versions of several scenes, and looked forward to seeing a live production. Everyone, that is, except Bill.

When I passed out the permission slips, he informed me that he would not be able to miss AP Biology, scheduled the same afternoon. Concerned, I met with Bill's biology teacher, who, after a lengthy discussion, gave Bill permission to attend the performance, even postponing classwork that Bill might be unable to do on his own. Pleased with her cooperation, I went back to Bill, who told me he still would not be attending.

"But you have to!" I unwisely shouted, up to my ears with his recalcitrance and exhausted from the extra work he had caused me.

"You can't make me miss AP Bio," he threatened.

"But your biology teacher said it's all right. You won't be missing anything you can't easily make up."

Stubbornly, Bill repeated, "I won't go. You can't make me. I'll ask my parents not to sign the permission slip. They'll call the principal."

And they did. Bill and I had finally met head on, and I had lost. Legally, I was told, I could not force Bill to see the play. So Lincoln Center brought an excellent production to central New Jersey that Bill never saw. When the teacher-artist returned the following day to lead Bill's class in an exchange about how their versions of several scenes compared to choices the director and actors from Lincoln Center had made, Bill "sat and listened." Aloof, he didn't want to be a group player. At least, not in our group.

A few months later, when I assigned an activity to write a group essay, Bill did play the game somewhat, albeit unhappily. Protesting, yet not wanting to jeopardize his grade substantially, he worked halfheartedly with three other group members, producing a mediocre paper, well below what he would have achieved alone. I reminded the class as we began that, in order to be successful in life, we must learn to work in groups and that there is much we can learn from others. But Bill, in his self-evaluation, asked, "What was the purpose of this? Do we have to do it again?" In answer to the question, "What are the needs, if any, of this paper?" Bill wrote, "There was not enough time allotted for the task. The class is not experienced enough in working in groups to do this. People have enough problems working with an editor. Four people *making one paper*, come on. . . . "

Although I was aware at the time that I had assigned an overly ambitious project, I was amazed to read, almost a year later, my antagonistic reply. "I'm sorry that you saw this task as 'much too difficult.' I'm not sure that you have a realistic expectation of the amount of work that a student should do in English. Perhaps you'll find this out in college." Obviously, I was pretty angry at Bill, but I didn't remember acknowledging this to myself at the time.

On the other hand, Bill was quite cooperative when I asked my students to choose the book they wanted to read from the various and sundry selections I brought to class. Bill chose Mary Shelley's *Frankenstein*. Two weeks later, he wrote a strong in-class essay about Shelley's concept of good and evil, beginning this way:

> We are brought into life helpless and unknowing, depending on our parents to teach us, to nurture us, and to let us learn from our experiences. We, as children, are naive and trusting of all, only seeking a soft, caressing voice to soothe our constant need

for love. Similar to the beliefs of the Romantics, man is born innately good and virtuous. But if there is a child born who is scorned and treated like an object of hate, that child will not look at society in a good way but will only learn to hate. The monster that Victor Frankenstein created was treated this way; it was the institutions of mankind that made him evil. This is shown throughout the novel which describes Mary Shelley's concept of good and evil.

Encouraged to pursue his own interests and work individually, Bill did fine. He remained inconsistent as a writer, however. What's more, he didn't want to hear about his work. He could not accept criticism, nor could he see himself critically. Although his strength was in his analytical work, for his final project Bill once again handed me an eight-stanza poem entitled "Life in General." The first stanzas follow:

With a slap and a scream,
*   We fulfill our parents' dreams.*
One which is filled with songs
*   And teachers preaching rights and wrongs.*
One with many faces to portray,
*   Which always come out to play.*
And thoughts of suicide
*   Which we always try to hide.*
And drugs and beer and wine
*   Which play games with our soul and mind.*

And a conscience that scares us more
*   Than any Forty-Second Street whore.*
And the concern about our appearance:
*   Which, in truth, doesn't make much sense.*
And the mistakes which are constantly made,
*   But, then again, experience means more than any grade.*
With bullies, punks, and the Boogy-Man,
*   Making us feel the need to run as fast as we can.*

My immediate reaction to Bill's final effort was to throw up my hands and moan, "What crap!" It wasn't until I reviewed Bill's work in preparation for this story that I saw "Life in

General" for what it was: a somewhat awkward attempt to write a poem about his own adolescent fears. Although I didn't realize it at the time, Bill was taking a chance, trying something new — what I had in fact asked him to do the previous September.

If I had seen Bill for who he was — an adolescent establishing his own identity — I would have been better able to teach him. Instead, I judged Bill self-centered and felt that he had an arrogant sense of his own superiority. What's more, I resented the fact that he challenged my control and resisted my comments. Bill was difficult, but he was also acting out a stage in his own life. As his teacher, I should have been more vigilant and gone that extra mile.

Our relationship never changed throughout Bill's senior year. Once again, in his course evaluation, he acted superior to the rest of the class and uncritical of his own work:

> I enjoyed the journal writing because it gave me a place to express my ideas where they would be appreciated and, especially, understood. What I mean is that having a discussion in this class has been completely different than the ones I had with the students who are in the AP class. It wasn't bad, but different.
>
> The literature that you chose was very helpful in understanding and learning more about myself, society, and the teachings that life has to offer. Writing poetry was what I liked most about this year, though. It let me express myself in an abstract way that made me think and confuse myself at the same time. I also think that poetry affects people differently than essays. Poems hit people harder while being subtle. I like that. I also feel that I'm good at writing poetry and will definitely continue writing in college.
>
> Overall, this year has changed my views on the English department in a positive way. I thank you for all you have done and wish you the best of luck in the future.

If I had been more perceptive, I might have realized that all the time I had thought Bill had shut me out, he had been listening. He just had not wanted to give me the pleasure of knowing I had had an effect on him. I wish I had been smarter. I might have gotten to know an interesting kid.

John

An Outsider Reaching In

John was the new guy on the block. Because of a job transfer, his family had left the Midwest the summer before he started his senior year. Although John was bright and good looking, he had not met many people. He was as shaky about his friendships as he was about his English skills. "We never had to do any writing in my other school," John told me, even before I announced the first assignment. "We just learned grammar and stuff. I never understood it, anyway." Although I was not sure whether or not to believe his excuses, John was quite candid about his insecurities.

I taught John's class during eighth period—the same period in which I taught Carol, Liz, and Jane, the last period of the day. Military history, the class John had before mine, was just across the hall. While his classmates hung out in front of my door, greeting their friends and making after-school plans until the last second before the bell rang, John always came right into class. It was during those four minutes of passing time alone with John that I began to get to know him: his shakiness, his sensitivity, his stubbornness, and his discomfort with his own feelings.

Luckily, John's class was the smallest I had: twenty seniors. They were all pretty good kids. Even though I followed the same lesson plans as with my earlier class, somehow things seemed more relaxed with John's group. It wasn't just that I had been through it once and knew the pitfalls. It may be that I was simply tired, and I tend to get silly when I'm tired. Fortunately, John's class seemed to respond positively to my relaxed attitude.

For the first autobiographical assignment, John chose to write about his father, entitling his paper "Love." Here is his final paragraph:

> There are many things I hope to be someday as a father. One of them is to be there, maybe not all the time, but really when my kids might need it. Try to help out in the little ways that kids don't notice. The ways that make you a better father and person. That is something my father gave which is so valuable, more than money or gifts, he gave of himself more than he knows.

John was right. He needed writing instruction, but not just in sentence structure. Nowhere in his paper did he describe his father; nowhere did he describe one thing that his father had done. There was no evidence in John's paper that his father "gave of himself more than he knows."

Along with other comments, I wrote, "You need to work on describing your father more fully — as an individual. How is he *different* from other good fathers?" John had weeks to think about this while he worked on his revision. But, two days before his final paper was due, he walked into the English office at the start of my Writing Lab duty for a conference that was to last forty-five minutes. John was stumped. For thirty-five minutes, he stubbornly protested that he didn't know how to improve his paper. For thirty-five minutes, I kept asking: "When did you and your father do things together?" "What are some examples of times when your father was there for you?" "Can you describe some of the little ways in which he helped you out?" "Can you tell me of a time when your father gave of himself?"

Ten minutes before the bell rang, John's face turned red and his eyes became darty. He looked as though he were about to explode. Nervously, I watched scarlet blotches cover his neck and spread below his open shirt collar. Finally, John mumbled tensely, between tight lips, "My father only spent time with me once. The tractor was broken. He asked me to help him fix it." The tension broken, we smiled wanly at each other as the bell rang. We went to our separate classes.

Two days later, John handed in his revision. At first glance, it was a total one, not seeming to resemble his initial paper in any way. In it, he told the truth. His dad was not the man who was always "there" for him. John's dad was not the man John wanted to be. In fact, his dad was the man John was afraid of becoming. What remained the same in his second paper was that John's dad was the man who was important to him — the man John loved. Here is his revised final paragraph:

> He won't ever know his entire influence over me, but I do. I know he gave me his smile and eyes, but underneath, he gave me more. Although he showed me how to work and how to cope with different situations, he also showed me that someone who thrives on stress will soon burn out. And that is where my father is now — riding the razor edge as if taunting the other side where depression lies like a monster. I realize that soon I could ride that same edge, but I hope that I, like my father should have, will learn to show my emotions and love.

John had taken the first steps to becoming a writer: digging down to the truth and having the courage to tell it. There is more than one way of looking at the truth, though, and from time to time John could even be playful, as he was in this satirical piece anticipating his own graduation party:

> Looking out the window, like the scarecrow looks out over the field, John watched as people began to wander away from his house. He could observe the people without them seeing him because of the sun shining off the glass.
>
> Music blared from his new stereo. It was a gift from one of his relatives, but at the time, he could not recall who gave it to him, nor did he care. He rocked to and fro with the beat of a song by Eddie Money "I Wanna Go Back."
>
> Off to the right, a knock coughed out from the other side of his door. He acknowledged nothing. The door opened a slight crack and then the crack enlarged quickly. Behind the door was John's mother. Although John got along with his mother it was a strained relationship, at times deteriorating into a tornado of arguing and defensive stances.

"Why don't you go downstairs and let your relatives see your bright, shining face? You know we didn't invite them here just so you could sit up in your room and listen to music," his mother said forcefully.

John raised his right eyebrow, but bit his tongue in order to avoid an argument that would mean little to him and was all but winnable. Slowly he rose and went over to the stereo and turned it off. As he reached the bottom step he looked for the sanctuary of a quiet corner. Finally, he found a place in the crowd, only remotely occupied by one other person, his father's boss.

"So, what kind of SAT's did you get?"

"I got a 1200," he answered dully. . . .

Sometimes, as on this occasion, John could laugh at himself, but most of the time he approached his writing from an intense and serious perspective. After discussing one of John's papers with him, I would often end up muttering to myself, "I'm an English teacher. Why does John make me feel like a therapist?"

After we read Hanley's *Slow Dance on the Killing Ground*, I asked John's section to respond with a project they would present to the class, interpreting an aspect of the play. I needed a respite from grading papers. The students also seemed to enjoy the change. They worked hard outside of class. Several students presented clay masks, explaining their artistic choices in terms of the characters they represented. A few talented art students made large posters depicting a scene from the play. Some read poems they had written about choices made by Hanley's characters. A trio even performed an original piece of music as an ensemble, each instrument the voice of a different actor. The students were excited about what they had accomplished, volunteering eagerly to come up in front of the class. All except John, who sat rigidly in the back of the room. Finally, he had no choice. There had been nineteen presentations; everyone knew it was his turn.

"What have you done?" the class asked him.

"It's nothing," John answered, clutching a crumpled plastic bag. "I'm good at history, but I can't do this kind of thing."

"Come on. Show it to us," the class cajoled. "We're not any good, but we did it."

After several minutes of this, John stiffly made his way to the front of the room, crumpled bag in hand. He sat himself on a chair in front of my desk, not on the desk, feet dangling, as other students had done. Slowly reaching into his bag, John pulled out a plaster mask that he had shaped to his face, then let dry.

The class gasped when they saw it. It was a sad, worried-looking mask, an older man's face, one who was confused and frustrated by life. John explained to us that it was Glas's face (a character in *Slow Dance* who felt as though his life was over). But John kept the mask in his lap while he talked. He didn't hold it up or let us look closely at it.

After John's presentation, even though he didn't seem to have anything more to say, he stayed at the front of the room, his face and neck again red and blotchy.

The class responded in a friendly way, complimenting him on his presentation. For the first time, John had communicated frankly to them; he was no longer hiding. When the bell rang, two students walked out of the room on either side of John, talking animatedly.

John's project had come from the bottom of that same crumpled bag from which he had brought out his essay on his father. He had dug down and come up with truth. In addition, what he came up with this time were nineteen new friends.

Shortly after this experience, I asked the class to count off to form heterogeneous groups in order to analyze two Wordsworth sonnets. They were then to write a group paper comparing and contrasting them. There were several class days to complete this, but because of the difficulty of the assignment, it required working together as a group outside of class as well.

Four of the groups managed to write acceptable papers. John's group wanted to do something different. I questioned them. Intrigued by their enthusiasm, I agreed to their proposal, even though they wanted their work to be a surprise:

simulating a broadcast about Wordsworth from England. John served as anchor person. Packed with historical research, his dateline captured the class's attention immediately. He then "went to Liz on location at Wordsworth's cottage." Liz regaled us with all kinds of tidbits about the poet himself. After further comments, John took us to London where Megan and Sue were "on location on Westminster Bridge." Sue interpreted one of the sonnets; Megan, the other. The class sat mesmerized for the entire period. Even more important, in their self-evaluations, each of the group members complimented the group as a whole, clearly establishing that the cooperative effort was greater than the sum of its parts. John was probably the most enthusiastic. He ended his self-evaluation by writing, "We are great!!!"

As the Beatles used to sing, John was learning to get by with a little help from his friends. Without his usual hesitations, he dug in and analyzed the sonnets. As his teacher, I was being taught that there were experiences, in addition to formal papers, that were important for developing writers.

Journal writing was another one of these experiences for John. While assigning some topics, I asked my seniors to write in the journal on their own as well. The following is an excerpt from John's journal: "They pull-n-push; try to manipulate me. Like a puppet I go through the motions. Being pulled by strings I am unchanged. As if a piece of wood with no feeling anymore. No goal. . . . "

The rhythms of John's language, the way he repeated the *p* sound, and the hollow marionette images his words evoked, made me want to line up this journal writing like poetry. When I did, it looked like this.

They pull push
Try to manipulate me
Like a puppet
I go through the motions

Pulled by strings
I am unchanged

A piece of wood
With no feeling anymore

Another excerpt from John's journal that I saw as an attempt to express the unexpressible is the following: "They say you should attain the world. But I am overwhelmed. Overwhelmed like that of a twig in a fast moving stream. Being pulled down a road of continual uproar. Friends are few, comrades are none. No one to talk to. Freedom I strive for, success'so close."

They say you should attain the world
But I am overwhelmed
Like a twig in a fast moving stream

Pulled down a road of continual uproar
Friends are few
Comrades are none

No one to talk to
Freedom I strive for
Success so close

John's journal was both honest and lyrical. Here he had no need for a teacher to say, "John, what do you really mean?"

John asked me if he could regularly turn in a journal. John's question really was, May I keep a journal instead of doing papers? I thought for a moment, and then replied, "Of course you can keep a journal, but you'll have to write papers, too." He smiled. That was fine with him.

John's journal writing carried over into his papers, as I had anticipated. By the end of the year, John showed that he could analyze a topic on his own. In answer to the self-evaluation question on his final paper "What did I try to improve or experiment with on this paper?" John replied, "I tried to use the journal that I had kept."

By spring, John was no longer showing up at Writing Lab the last minute before a paper was due. He was no longer as insecure about his friendships or his English skills. Sensitive and stubborn, John was only beginning to feel comfortable with his own feelings, yet he had taken some valid steps on his own toward becoming a writer. John was far from the best writer in that senior class, but he may have progressed the furthest.

Reflections

My relationship with Bill was different from my relationship with Jeremy and John. With Bill, I was more distant. I never became a trusted adult. In my classroom, Bill never became an invested writer. Jeremy and John did. Sometime during the course of the year, they began to trust me. They committed themselves to telling the truth, which in my mind is the first step toward becoming a writer. The truth is hard to write. When writers attempt to tell the truth, their work takes on another dimension. Jeremy and John found this out.

And so have I. But what I know as a writer I have had to learn as a teacher. Arguing with Jeremy, I had not tried to play the role of an authority figure. Helping John dig down to find the truth, my overall concerns had been greater than the outcome of his paper. I allowed Jeremy and John to see more than Mrs. Lott, the teacher. Each time I slipped off my teacher's mask and became truly myself, my existence in that factory-like building we call "high school" became more bearable.

Even so, Part Five of this book is evidence that I have continued to change. My husband, who has been teaching history for thirty years, continuously alters his material. "I've never taught the course the same way from one year to the next," he tells me proudly. Perhaps that is why he is still enthusiastic about his job.

I introduced portfolios into my classroom because I wanted my students to become more involved in their own writing. As Ann Berthoff (1987) says, to "give them back their language" (p. 38). I wanted them to have the opportunity "to begin again," to have the option to change and grow. And I wanted to assess them in a more equitable fashion, given their diverse skills and maturity levels.

When I began to use portfolios, it was as though I had raised an imaginary window in room C102: the air seemed fresher. My students chose the papers they wanted to continue to revise; they had time to reflect; they played with language, making "many starts." My students accomplished work that mattered to them.

And so did I. My teaching life and my writing life began to connect. I no longer felt fragmented. Finally, I was teaching what I had known, as a writer, all along.

Part Five

Using Portfolios

Our students can learn to write only if we give them back their language, and that means playing with it, working with it, using it instrumentally, making many starts. We want them to learn the truth of Gaston Bachelard's observation that "in the realm of the mind, to begin is to know you have the right to begin again."

— Ann E. Berthoff, 1987

Chris

Quitting the Honor Student Game

*I*n order to introduce the concept of portfolios, I gave my students the following handout the first day of school, and suggested that they show it to their parents:

Grades each marking period will be given on the basis of portfolios. Although we will be doing a great amount of writing in this course—much of it on topics of particular interest to you—none of it will be graded except for your portfolio. Instead, you will be given teacher and peer comments, along with editing instruction. The fact that you have completed the assignment will be recorded; it will be impossible to pass this course with incomplete assignments.

At the end of each marking period, you will turn in a portfolio for a grade. Included in this portfolio will be two or three pieces of writing which you have selected. Since *you* will have chosen these works, I will expect them to be important—essays, stories, or poems that you have made an effort to perfect. All drafts of these pieces along with any comments you have received will also be included. Your grade will be based on the quality of work in your portfolio, on the progress you have made from original draft to final portfolio piece, and on the risks you have taken.

In addition, you will include in your portfolio an introductory essay explaining why you have chosen the pieces in it, the progress you see that you have made in your writing, and what you still want to accomplish. In this reflective essay, it will also be appropriate to discuss your own writing process—the circumstances in which you write and the history of your writing practices. If you have questions about your writing or want a particular response to anything you have written, say so in this introduction.

As your teacher, my concern is to help *you* improve your writing, to be your ally. Not until you hand in your portfolio, will I be your judge. Again, my judgment will be based on your effort, the quality of your work, and your introductory essay. My hope is to see you grow, to see your writing improve, and to prepare you for college. None of this can be accomplished without real effort on your part.

Students could select from their writing the pieces they most wanted to revise for the portfolio they were required to hand in each marking period. By questioning themselves, they no longer had to ask, What does the *teacher* want? Instead, they could begin to inquire, What's important to *me?* to become more engaged in their own work.

It fascinated me to discover that students who would normally get A's in senior year would have to work harder when evaluated by portfolios than by traditional assessment measures.

Christopher's story exemplifies this. Although Chris was a talented student, he let me know rather quickly that he didn't care about English; science was his interest. He had ambitions to be either a doctor or an engineer. Because he was taking AP science and math courses, Chris wanted a course to coast through. Portfolios, though, made his coasting through English impossible.

Chris expressed this realization in the reflective essay that introduced his portfolio in the first marking period:

> I probably spent more time this quarter on writing English papers than ever before. Before taking this class, I would merely weed out my mechanical errors while typing my single draft of a paper on the computer. My thinking and writing process has always been slow, but now I am writing several drafts of each paper, each one better than the last after self, peer, and teacher editing.

No longer able to get away with a single draft or secure in the knowledge that his effort would earn him an A, he was "writing several drafts of each paper," aware that "each one

[was] better than the last." For the first time in an English class, Chris was not only being challenged, but he was also challenging himself. An able student whose concern had been confined to the sciences, Chris was now, through his own efforts, becoming interested in the humanities. He desired to "mature mentally and emotionally" through his writing. In this same essay, Chris wrote that he wanted to grow as a writer and a person.

> Perhaps as a result of this extra time spent, my writing is improving. I am now experimenting with interest catchers to begin my papers. I can see how some of my previous work must have been quite dull without them. I am also now better able to prove a point in a paper. I have never had any real problem with organization, but I never seemed to be able to explain my examples enough. As you can see between the various drafts of my "graduate" paper I am overcoming my subconscious assumption that the reader has an identical thought process to mine.
>
> However, I am still not able to dig too far below the surface in my interpretations. I need to improve my analyzing skills, not just for literature or movies, but for my own personal thoughts and feelings. I realize not all emotions can be explained rationally, but I have trouble explaining why I think this or why I feel that, no matter what the subject is. Although I have become much more in touch with my emotions over the past year, the detachment that remains still shows up as a weakness in my writing.
>
> This is the first year I ever seriously worried about the quality of my writing, and I hope this ambition will help me in my quest for improvement. This ambition is not only coming from a procrastinated desperation to be able to write good college essays, but also from a genuine concern and belief that I can mature mentally and emotionally if I can put more feeling into my writing.

How did I know that Chris wasn't just playing the honor student game of trying to please me, that expressing a desire to "mature mentally and emotionally" wasn't a way to impress his teacher? There had to be some of that; there always is. The difference, though, was that Chris and I both could see evidence of his progress in the portfolio he had arranged. One of the entries he concentrated on the first marking period was his film analysis paper. As Chris pointed out in the reflective essay that introduced his portfolio, "I am overcoming my subconscious assumption that the reader has an identical thought process to mine." He was learning how and when to explain his examples. He was also experimenting with his writing. For the revision of his film analysis of *The Graduate*, he chose to test an expanded conclusion, something I had recently taught in class. His original conclusion follows:

> Whether the viewers realize it consciously or not, film techniques such as arrangement, camera angles, and lighting can be used just as effectively as plot and dialogue to prove a point or present an idea or image in a film. In "The Graduate," director Mike Nichols succeeds in using film techniques to show Mrs. Robinson's initial domination over Ben and her loss of this control as Ben gains power during the film.

I pointed out to him that, although acceptable, his conclusion was a simple summary. I wondered if he could take it a step further. Since Chris began this same paper with a quotation from "Ruthless Bitch" by Tairrie B. (Comptown/MCA Records), I suggested he could refer back to that if he liked. Here is the expanded conclusion as presented in his first-quarter portfolio:

> Whether the viewers realize it consciously or not, film techniques such as arrangement, camera angles, and lighting can be used just as effectively as plot and dialogue to prove a point or present an idea or image in a film. In "The Graduate," director Mike Nichols succeeds in using film techniques to show Mrs. Robinson's initial domination over Ben and her loss of this control as Ben gains power during the film. Mrs. Robinson, however, is not the only character to lose command over Ben. Ben's parents had been telling him what to do and how to do it his entire life, and Mr. Robinson is easily able to dominate a conversation with Ben.

Nichols does not stress Ben's relationship in terms of power with these characters as much as his relationship with Mrs. Robinson, yet there is sufficient evidence to suggest that Ben begins the film as a subservient underling to each and ends up independent of and even rebellious toward these former authority figures. At the end of the film, Ben has matured into a male BITCH by Being In Total Control of HIMself and refusing to take orders from anyone.

Even though the original conclusion was satisfactory, Chris was required to show progress in his portfolio. By expanding his conclusion and circling back to his introduction, he broadened his repertoire and grew mentally as a writer. Emotional growth, though, is more difficult to specify. Nevertheless, Chris attempted to do so in his portfolio during the second marking period, as suggested in the following selection:

One of my major goals for writing this quarter, as I stated in my last reflective essay, was to be able to put more feeling into my writing. I have succeeded at least partially in achieving this goal. My college essay and personal reaction to Wordsworth's "Ode: Intimations of Immortality" might not be one of the best papers I have written, but the fact that I could write entire papers based on my own thoughts and feelings impressed me. This is something I have never really done before. It was exciting to see my printer churn out for the first time three full pages of uninhibited Christopher Smith.

I can still remember times when I had difficulty writing a three page research paper, when my own opinion was not required or even wanted. My problem has progressed from organizing other people's opinions to organizing my own. For now, though, I am satisfied with just being able to acknowledge my own thoughts and feelings. I had never really had to do any writings "from the heart" until recently, so it is just now that I am coming to terms with a problem that has been with me for years. I used to repress my inner emotions, fearing that since they were probably different from those of my peers, I might become a social outcast if they were known. I shuddered at the thought of having even a single enemy, so I always considered the consequences before I acted or spoke. Now that I can stand up for what I believe in, I feel much better about myself, and I do not really care what other people think of me. Perhaps this sentiment is most adequately described by my favorite rapper Ice Cube, who says, "You don't like how I'm livin' well fuck you."

So I have progressed greatly this quarter by becoming even more in touch with my emotions and being able to organize them somewhat on the written page. I still need to define my feelings a little more clearly, since some of them still seem to either contradict the others or just plain make no sense. I also need to greatly improve the organization of these thoughts in my writing, and to add some complexity to the language in which I write about myself. It seems the deeper I dig into myself to write on a given subject, the simpler the language becomes—I guess down deep I am just a simple person. My writing is in the transition phase, far from perfect, but my progress thus far certainly looks promising.

Chris's personal reaction to Wordsworth's ode was, as he expressed it, an "entire [paper] based on [his] own thoughts and feelings. . . ." In two separate aspects of this paper, Chris was able to demonstrate how he had grown emotionally. When he began writing, Chris had ignored some of his own experience. The second paragraph of one of the earlier drafts in his portfolio demonstrates this.

My childhood, like Wordsworth's, was a blissful one. "Every common sight, / To me did seem/ Appareled in celestial light." I was awed by the wonders of nature and life. As I grew accustomed to these new sights over time, however, my amazement began to gradually decrease. Wordsworth describes a similar situation in which "there (passes) away a glory from the earth" as he loses contact with his spiritual self. I have gone a step further away from my soul than Wordsworth has at this point, though, since I am now in a phase of doubting whether my soul was ever present to lose. My acquisition of knowledge over the years since my early childhood brought about this doubtfulness.

Comments Chris received on this draft suggested that he describe some of the sights of his childhood. He responded, and in doing so, he became less restrained.

My childhood, like Wordsworth's, was a blissful one. "Every common sight, / To me did seem/ Appareled in celestial light." I was awed by the wonders of nature and life. More than anything else I enjoyed getting lost in the woods, wading in muddy creeks, and climbing trees. Animals especially fascinated me, and I was always trying to catch and make a pet out of some wild creature, be it a crayfish, turtle, snake, or bird. I enjoyed myself outdoors much more so than indoors and felt truly at one with nature. As I grew accustomed to these new sights over time, however, my amazement began to gradually decrease. Wordsworth describes a similar situation in which "there [passes] away a glory from the earth" as he loses contact with his spiritual self. I have gone a step further away from my soul than Wordsworth has at this point, though, since I am now in a phase of doubting whether my soul was ever present to lose. My acquisition of knowledge over the years since my early childhood brought about this doubtfulness.

This was not the only aspect of growth on Chris's part, however. As he had written in his reflective essay, Chris was now "able to acknowledge [his] own thoughts and feelings." Feelings about his parents' divorce were among these, but in one of his earlier drafts of this same essay, he only alluded to the event:

As I grew older, I learned more from school and books, taking a particular interest in science. My curiousity grew: I wanted to know how and why things happened. I learned more about pre-history, dinosaurs, cavemen, fossils, carbon-14 dating, even evolution. I cannot recall precisely when the religion-contradicts-science revelation dawned on me, but it was near the time of my parents' divorce, a major turning point in my life at eleven years. There was much doubt in my mind about God and religion, but religion was still not to be questioned. I wanted to be like everyone else, so I held my tongue and pretended to believe. I hoped perhaps one day God would decide to come to me and explain, or would perform some miracle to reaffirm my waning faith.

Reading this draft, one of Chris's peer editors asked him how his loss of faith in God was connected to his parents' divorce. When Chris showed this comment to me, I pointed out to him that earlier in his paper, describing his religious training, he had written, "Yet from the definition of God I was taught, He may as well be my parents." Pondering this, Chris produced the following revision:

> As I grew older, I learned more from school and books, taking a particular interest in science. My curiousity grew: I wanted to know how and why things happened. I learned more about pre-history, dinosaurs, cavemen, fossils, carbon-14 dating, even evo-lution. I cannot recall precisely when the religion-contradicts-science revelation dawned on me, but it was near the time of my parents' divorce, a major turning point in my life at eleven years. Although I do not specifically recall the details of my inner thoughts at this time, it seems logical that my loss of faith in God may well have been connected to my parents' separation. How could a truly benevolent God in Heaven sit back and allow some-thing as painful and emotionally trying as this to happen to me? What had I done to deserve such a harsh punishment? No God would put me through this kind of suffering for no apparent rea-son. I therefore became disillusioned with God and religion. However, I still wanted to be like everyone else, so I held my tongue and pretended to believe. I hoped perhaps one day God would decide to come to me and explain, or would perform some miracle to reaffirm my waning faith.

Chris had certainly judged himself accurately in his reflec-tive essay. He had "progressed greatly by becoming even more in touch with [his] emotions and being able to organize them." What particularly pleased me, though, was Chris's level of involvement. He was beginning to see himself as a writer, not only as a scientist. Would this same excitement have been manifest if he hadn't written "from the heart"? A complicated question. Writing "from the heart" hadn't been one of my requirements. Perhaps because Chris was really engaged in his writing for the first time, he saw this involve-ment as heartfelt. Now, brave enough not to "consider the consequences" before he wrote, Chris had stopped editing himself out before he even began. For the first time as an

English student, he was excited with "full pages of uninhibited Christopher Smith."

Portfolios had an unexpected effect on Chris. Reflecting on his writing, he realized how some feelings or ideas "seem to either contradict others or just plain make no sense." And like Siddhartha, whose journey ended by the river, Chris saw that "deep down" he was just "a simple person." If I had continued to evaluate single papers, this might not have happened. Using portfolios, Chris had the opportunity to reflect and the option to change and grow. He also discovered that writing can be as amazing as science.

Teena

A Poet's Portfolio

Unlike Chris, Teena, a junior, had always loved to write. Her pale skin glowed when, brushing her red hair out of her eyes, she talked to me about poetry. Teena and Chris's dissimilarity stopped there, though. Teena had also achieved in English, evaluated by more traditional methods. And unfortunately, she, too, had not been totally engaged in her writing. Working with portfolios, however, prevented Teena from fragmenting her creative energy. She could work on a project that was important to her inside the classroom as well as out. More in charge of her own learning, she was content in school, expressing this in the reflective essay that introduced her first marking period's portfolio.

In the past, when I looked over my work from the beginning of the year, I felt really stupid. It's not that I made drastic advancement; it's just that I found it difficult to believe I ever produced such trash. This year, now that I'm examining my portfolio, I'm not too disturbed. I'm happy with all my work—so far. Although when I neglected to follow directions on our first assignment on summer reading, I thought I'd die. But I didn't. I just revised it and now it's in the portfolio. Life goes on.

I really appreciated the comments on the *Catcher in the Rye* essay. They helped me a lot. I always enjoy writing most when it is left up to me to choose what I'm writing about. This freedom gives me the opportunity to work on a subject that interests me; therefore, I get more involved in my work. Thanks for trusting us with the choice of a topic. I had a great time with the aspect of false bravado and society's expectations of man. Satisfied with my paper and grade, I agree with your suggestion to discuss women in the paper as well. I think I've just overcome my "five paragraph essay" fixation. . . .

. . . I believe that the main reason for my contentment with my work so far this year is my level of involvement. I can't imagine anything more appetizing than the option to explore what interests me or to express myself in the manner most comfortable. The result of this option is work I enjoy putting effort into. All the work I have done has been important to me, something I care about. I live for this. I am anticipating a terrific year.

In this introductory essay, Teena gave several reasons why portfolios were of value. First of all, she said that she was able to choose what was important to her. She didn't have to look back, feeling "stupid" or thinking her work was "trash." Secondly, she realized that if she initially made a mistake, as she did on her first assignment, she could rectify it without wanting to "die." In addition, she could change her approach to an essay and experiment with new forms, thereby overcoming her "five-paragraph essay fixation." The most important benefit to Teena, though, was that portfolios increased her "level of involvement." Teena already cared about her writing and liked to work independently. Completing a portfolio over the course of a marking period allowed her to connect her outside interests to the work she was doing in school. Rereading the opening paragraph of the *Catcher in the Rye* essay that Teena referred to in her introduction, I could feel her pleasure:

"Go ahead, make my day," uttered with such jarring simplicity and chilling confidence no one has yet dared to contest this infamous quote credited to Clint Eastwood. A steely gaze, a low, throaty voice and Mr. Eastwood has established himself as "man." This level of unpenetrable masculinity seems too good to be true. However, society assures us that this—this whiskey-drinking, square jaw-twitching, thin-lipped sneering, body of stone—this is "man." Perhaps it is so, but I doubt it. Experience with more realistic characters leads me to believe that there is more depth to the theory of "man." This case of false bravado may be particularly true in the instance of J.D. Salinger's character, Holden Caulfield, in *The Catcher in the Rye*.

137

Playing with language, Teena poked fun at the "whiskey-drinking, square jaw-twitching, thin-lipped sneering, bod[ies] of stone" Clint Eastwood portrayed. She was able to put all her energy into her work. Teena expressed this in a letter to me, which served as the introduction to her portfolio for the second marking period.

Dear Mrs. Lott,

... To begin with, of the three required works, I have included two poems. Why? The reason is that you requested the three works to be accurate reflections of ourselves and our potential. I thought of compiling a traditionally well-rounded portfolio including the standard poem, short story/descriptive, and expository essay. Then I said to myself, "Teena, life is just too sweet to be so boring." Thus, I present to you an untraditional, yet accurate reflection of me....

... The second poem I have included is in a different voice. I am no longer using a tone of raw logic, but focusing on creating an experience for the reader. When writing anything, my favorite part of the process is choosing words. In my poem about the heat of the night I selected the ones that I think fit perfectly. A lot of times I worry myself when I realize I'm having a better time thinking up juicy words than I have on some Saturday nights. It really is scary. I revised this poem (without changing any important words, only prepositions and such) with the usage of space in mind. How I set up a poem is relevant to what I'm communicating. However, when I'm equally content expressing an idea several different ways I end up with several different versions.

And so I come to my short story/descriptive. Even though this form is not my strong point, I liked this assignment. In my last portfolio I told you how much I appreciated the freedom in choosing topics. Although I am less comfortable writing in this form, being able to choose my topic made the story less painful to compose. I have found that I am blissfully content writing in any style as long as I like what I'm writing about. The preparations for this assignment were also helpful. The time spent in class free writing and doing associations was time well spent. It organized my thoughts and inspired my writing. I have revised my "Blankie" story using many of your suggestions and a few ideas of my own.

So this is my portfolio. It sums up my accomplishments so far this year. English has always been a favored subject of mine; however, it has never been so consistently enjoyable for me. I love being interested in what I'm doing. Then I apply myself to my work....

Teena thrived on the freedom arranging a portfolio offered. As long as she fulfilled all her assignments, she could work on her poetry, which was what she really wanted to do. While compiling her portfolio and analyzing her selections, Teena had the opportunity to reflect on her writing process. She could consider how she wrote a poem and why she made the choices she did. The "second" poem Teena referred to in her reflective essay is an example of the strength of her work.

> *the heat of the night*
> *when the air is so parched*
> > *it begins to crack*
> *and scorched smells of outside*
> > *wander in*
> *on non-existent*
> > *breaths of wind*
> *the baked in warmth of day*
> > *burns my throat*
> *I lie*
> > *sweltering*
> > > *unable to escape*
> *the heat of the night*

But since one of the selections in her portfolio was mandatory, Teena also was required to work in an area in which she was not so strong. Doing this, she could reflect on just what processes now made a previously difficult form — "short story/ descriptive" — easier for her to accomplish. The way Teena expressed it, her ace in the hole was choosing her own topic. Asked to describe an event that changed her life, Teena wrote about the time she left Blankie, her baby blanket, in nursery school:

Nursery school was the answer to my Romp-a-Room dreams. Finger-painting and dot-to-dots were perfectly satisfying and enjoyable pastimes for me. How could I argue with the cheerful multi-colored rooms, every toy and game available, and an outdoor playground (sandbox included)? Never had I had any complaints about nap-time either, until a day that is still accurately etched into my memory. That day I had brought Blankie in for show-and-tell. I was particularly anticipating nap-time due to the fact Blankie and I would be able to relish each other's company to full potential in this environment. It was bliss. However, at the end of the day, I inexcusably forgot Blankie in my cubby. The real crisis occured, though, when my once endeared nursery school teachers refused to permit me to ever bring Blankie home again. . . .

Teena contined — detailing her reactions, her rescue plan, and what ensued at home:

Nothing could stop me, not until my demands were met. My parents, the good people they are, tried everything. Every blanket in our entire house was laid at my feet to substitute for the absent Blankie. Every blanket in our house was thrown to the floor with shrieks of outrage. I remember crying so hard and long that my head was pounding and my hair was damp with perspiration. Offered every possible object of desire to compensate my loss, I refused them all.

In these excerpts from her "Blankie" narrative, Teena demonstrated that she was just as careful as she had been in her poem about her choice of words. "Blissfully content," she was happy "writing in any style as long as [she] like[d] what [she] was writing about."

Everything Teena felt passionate about — "Saturday nights," "juicy words," and setting up a poem that was relevant to what she wanted to communicate — could be included in her portfolio. And using portfolios, Teena became totally engaged in her writing.

Timothy

A Diamond in the Rough

In November, I read a speech I was writing about portfolios to my fifth-period class. "You might be bored," I warned them. "My audience is teachers and teachers-in-training. I need your help, though. I want you to listen and tell me, from your point of view, whether or not I'm telling the truth." In a week I planned to speak about portfolios at the National Council of Teachers of English (NCTE) conference. I didn't want to say anything that was not so.

"What you wrote is true," they told me. Your writing is boring, though. Sorry, Mrs. Lott. No offense. I mean, why don't you include your audience more? Ask them what they think. Things like that."

A little defensively, I agreed. "Do you have any suggestions, though? Is there anything I should add or leave out?"

My fifth-period students shook their heads. Except for Timothy. Coolly, from his seat in the back of the room, he asked, "Mrs. Lott, why didn't you mention creativity?"

I thought that creativity had been implicit in what I had written, especially in Teena's story, but perhaps I hadn't emphasized it enough. Timothy's portfolio had certainly been an example of creativity. Talented in art, disruptive at the fall pep rally, sporting army boots and ponytail, Timothy was the oddball creative kid par excellence who hated school.

But Timothy liked portfolios. His introductory reflective essay from his first portfolio explains why.

The quarter that has just passed was a rollercoaster: I hit each peak and each valley at the least 200 times . I believed it to be the cause of college and schoolwork related stress .THe only way I coped was by writing and painting . I was delighted to write in your class and wish we could do more . Everything I wrote this quarter was extremely close to me ; I lived or felt each thing . I treat writing like drawing and painting now so it was very important to me .

I was pleased with my project last symester . I enjoyed the descriptive and sarcastic style in my papers and the symbolism and emotion that was displayed in my poetry . THe fact that I cared about what I wrote made the writing process more gratifying. THe writing was a great release, like a hot shower when your body aches .I, indeed, appreciate the humor in my writing, in the process of essay composing but I also savor the depression or despair that comes out of poetry . Its a chance to get the "blues" out of my system.

The definite weakness in my writing was disorganization of ideas and grammer.I believe that I should in my case write an outline of my ideas ; not to get so mixed up in my thoughts . In all my papers I had to rewrite in the midlle; do to unorganized thoughts. The other fault was grammer. I would constanly spell words wrong like grammar , which made me look like a fool . Grammar involves a lot of structire . I hated structure and my sentences proved it . They were filled with sentence fragments and obscurity .I should relearn my grammar rules before I go to college .that was what I loved about painting ; no structure .

The works I chose for the portfolio are as follows ; 'The Man , the Legend , Walter Gearon', an essay , 'Man Leaps His Night' , a poem and 'Lost' , an unassigned poem . They all contained the emotions within me that needed to be expressed . I was proud of my essay because it contained the style I love to write in: descriptive and sarcastic . I felt I was successful in my attempt to show my father as my role model . And the way I used his cursing and my art work to be one in the same enthused me . I thought I executed it wall . THe essay was fun but it did suck writing all those damn copies. . . .

. . . I worked extra hard on my portolio this quarter and I expect a lot back . I never put so much time into preparing projects and so much heart .I am content with my choices for the portfolio and they represent my peak in writing . I hope you have a fun time grading my work and I'll see you in a week .

Timothy had conscientiously followed my advice: "Revise your work on a word processor. If you can't get to one, use a typewriter." It was obvious, though, that he still had not had much experience spacing or finding keys on a keyboard. My lenses get stronger each year as a result of straining over so much student writing, but the motivation behind my requirement was not only to preserve my eyesight. I wanted my students to have a sense of completion, to feel, in a way, as though they had published.

Timothy struck some wrong keys, misspelled some words, misused or forgot to use some apostrophes, and needed some help with punctuation. But, even if Timothy's mistakes had been careless ones, I was still convinced that he cared about his reflective essay. Timothy wrote in it that he was treating writing "like drawing and painting now." Writing had become something that mattered to him. When I returned Timothy's portfolio, I argued that painting also involved "structure," but after writing Billy's story, I made the decision that teaching is not about proving you're right.

I guess you would have had to have seen Timothy — his laced-up black boots, hair that was long in the back and shaved on the sides, his inquiring blue eyes — to feel the way I did when I read, "The writing was a great release, like a hot shower when your body aches." I felt as pleased as Timothy that he had had "a chance to get the 'blues' out of [his] system."

My reaction to Timothy's statement, "I worked extra hard on my portfolio this quarter and I expect a lot back," was more complex. I had to take a careful look at Timothy's work to see if this statement was a challenge, a ploy, or a sincere admission.

Timothy's first portfolio piece was "The Man, the Legend, Walter Gearon." It began this way:

"Those goddamned sunna ofa bitchin bastards, those submoronic fools, they will give me indigestion!", exclaimed my father in a low alto voice, as he smacked his tan semi-wrinkled forehead with a sweat bead that dripped down the side of his face in one breath.

Without a doubt in my young mind, my father has just returned from the most disorganized place of trade in the world, the A & P, or as known in the Gearon house, HELL! The store, once again, made my father wait an extra excruciating fifteen minutes in line, because they only had one, that is right, one, express lane open. "Those goddamned bastards, Jesus Christ, just Christ fifteen minutes!" my father uttered incoherently again, with a purple-pink vein popping out above his eye utilizing a rythimic beat. I, of course, tried to maintain the beat by playing my homemade drum kit. Ingredients are as follows: two pencils ten inches in length, and a brown solid oak kitchen table. After the outburst, my father dropped to the couch and slowly drifted off into Walter land.

He stood five feet ten inches, or eleven heads high, and his hair, which was thinning, was dark brown with tints of gray intermixed, to give him that neo-father of the forties look. His luggage or skin was deep brown, but only on his forearms and head. Otherwise he was pale white; he suffered from an acute case of farmers' tan. That day he was wearing baggy light blue slacks, with orange golf dirt stuck to his cuffs, with a white polo shirt that had a pack of smokes in the pocket, and a burgandy wind breaker that he picked up in Greenwich Village, N.Y.; a modern day Andy Warhol.

My father, or master of the monologue, performed to the zenith that day. It was a religious experience more powerful than when Jesus walked on water. After his soliloquy, he had fallen asleep, like he had just engaged in hardcore sex. He had a smile ear to ear on his face while he slept the afternoon goodbye. When he awoke, the giddy school boy danced quite elegantly around the family room. He looked at me while putting MC HAMMER to shame and said, "Give me convenience or give me death!" I have no idea what he was talking about. I remember saying to myself, "so it goes. . . . "

Attached to Timothy's essay were his drafts. For his first draft, he had jotted notes about the requirements for the essay — "Organize your essay around framework," "One tone," "Interesting opening sentence," through "Tie piece together" — in a column that curved down the right-hand side of a piece of notebook paper. These notations were the result of an in-class lecture I had given in order to describe the assignment.

After I had finished discussing requirements, I modeled clustering (a brainstorming strategy that graphically represents associations between a focused topic and the writer's personal associations) on the board for the class. Timothy turned this same piece of notebook paper horizontally and placed the name of his father, "Walter Gearon," in a bubble on the lefthand side of the page. Drawing a line from the bubble, Timothy wrote: "He wear a grayishyellow walking shoes with brown socks and blue pants when he golfs." Then at the top of the page, just to the right of a Henry Moore-like drawing of a boy and his father, Timothy scribbled, "Tells me to think positive." Timothy also jotted down, "smokes the hardest cigarette around—A quality of a real man smoker." Just to the right of this clustering, Timothy scrawled what was to become, in slightly different form, his opening paragraph, "Open with the time he forgot the luncheon meats at A&P."

The day after I introduced this assignment to my students, I asked them to make columns on a separate sheet of paper in their notebook: "physical appearance," "clothing," "personality traits," "idiosyncrasies," "habits," "hobbies," "likes," "dislikes," "childhood," "education," "jobs," and "mannerisms." These headings were not original. They came from a helpful book on teaching autobiography, *I Remember: An Autobiography Text for High School Students* (Francine G. Wacht, 1986), which I had used previously for this project.

Timothy made his notations on the far left-hand side of the page. Most of Timothy's comments were listed horizontally; a few were listed in slanted vertical columns; and three were listed upside-down. Clearly, Timothy was going to write about his father in his own fashion. Some of Timothy's notations were repetitive. Timothy wrote "curses like the Dickins" under his father's hobbies and repeated "curses well" under his father's idiosyncrasies. This torn-out notebook page appeared in Timothy's portfolio as his second draft.

After completing this exercise, Timothy began to write his paper with his father's exclamations—"Those goddamed sunna of a bitchin bastards. They do not do one fuckin thing . . . :" As a lead-in to his father's complaints, Timothy had written at the top of the page, "'Expression of feelings is critical in living a non repressed life'. This quote illustrates away of life for many artists in many fields." Timothy had crossed out on second thought the finale of his opening, "That includes my father and myself."

Timothy's next step was to read his essay aloud to his writing group. He recorded some of their comments at the bottom of what he considered to be his third draft. "Timothy state you learned to express yourself" and "Try to explain your father," his classmates suggested. After listening to his peers, Timothy worked through several more drafts of his essay before he handed his paper in to me for comments.

After reading my comments, Timothy made some changes on the same paper he had handed in, using asterisks. He also wrote a rather telling and humorous note to himself at the top, which he enclosed in a border, "Mrs lott suggest something, do it." As independent as Timothy appeared, he was aware that I would be the one to ultimately grade his portfolio.

My guess is that Timothy got someone who knew keyboarding better than he did to reproduce the final version of "The Man, The Legend, Walter Gearon." Timothy's paper appeared to be a pretty professional job. After reading Timothy's other two selections, I wrote him a note and graded his portfolio. I told Timothy that I did, in fact, have "fun" reading his work, as he had hoped, and that it was obvious from his portfolio that he had "worked extra hard."

The following week, when I returned portfolios to my fifth-period class, we formed a circle. I asked each of the students to read something aloud from his or her portfolio. I watched Timothy's pale face, under his black wool hat, light up when he glanced at my remarks. Confidently, Timothy read, "The Man, The Legend, Walter Gearon." After he finished, the fifth-period senior class applauded—spontaneously.

Having taught Timothy the year before, I recognized how important this applause must have been to him. In one of his long poems junior year, he had written:

... I built a wall
Noone would be allowed in,
I was scared that they'd no me,
The steel wall would run my depressed life.
I wouldn't try to take a chance,
My proud days were all lost,
Nowhere to be seen. ...

Timothy not only desired acceptance by peers, though his appearance might belie it, he also wanted to be accepted by his teachers. Because of my emphasis on grades junior year, Timothy had had a hard time. In November of that year, he wrote me the following letter:

Dear Mrs. Lott,

I'm writing this letter to you because I'm concerned about my grades. I'm not used to getting d's and f's. I know you are not at fault and I am, but its still hard for me to swallow.

Regarding the last essay that I writ, I was angry. You see, I can't type. It took me 3 hours to just type 2 pages. When you say, I hope you can type it over, it upsets the hell out of me. I don't have 3 to 4 hours to dish out on your class. ...

Junior year, Timothy's mother and I conferred about his writing problems. We were concerned about his spelling and lack of organization but weren't sure if testing Timothy for learning disabilities was the proper route. Regardless, I suggested that he take a typing course over the summer.

Just a few months ago, Timothy's mother requested a second conference. Both she and I were enthusiastic about his progress senior year. "What do you attribute it to?" I asked her.

"Portfolios," she replied without hesitation. "He loves them. He's less nervous and tense when he writes now. He tells me that he doesn't have to worry about his grade until the end of the marking period."

"That's right," I nodded.

Grinning from ear to ear, I realized that Timothy wasn't the only one who felt better about himself.

Reflections

Stephen D. Brookfield, professor of adult education at Columbia University, spoke at a college forum series for Thomas Edison State College in New Jersey, describing a pattern in adult learning that he called "incremental fluctuation." I realized that I had witnessed this same learning pattern — with myself and with high school students. "When we learn, we take two steps forward, one step backward and continue to make progress this way, in a zigzag pattern," Brookfield said. "This pattern may start with enthusiasm for learning, only to hit a block where the student may experience disappointment or frustration. After this initial setback, a new realization or wave of enthusiasm may occur, propelling the student forward in the learning process." By looking at portfolios, rather than individual papers, both students and teachers can see evidence of forward movement even as part of this zigzag pattern.

Using portfolios, I could see other changes, also. As my students became more absorbed in their own writing, the classroom environment subtly changed. Slowly, the emphasis shifted from pleasing the teacher and writing for grades to making choices and taking risks. An informality developed, almost a workshop-like atmosphere. I was no longer the one in control. More often than not, we formed a circle or scattered around the room rather than remaining in rows with me at the head. From time to time, I shared my own writing with students, and a climate of trust developed.

Some students were involved in long-term projects that required sustained interest and independent effort for the first time. This caused them to take a more active role in their own learning. "May I read my piece to the class?" they would ask as soon as they entered the room. Not only did most students share their work aloud, but they began to respond in writing to literary texts, also reading these responses orally.

Developing ground rules as we went along, we often felt like explorers in new territory. As we inquired, we found that some approaches worked better than others. Therefore, in no way do I want to suggest that my method of working with portfolios should be duplicated by colleagues. This would be as dangerous as stating that there is *one* writing process.

What Worked for Us

At a given point in the portfolio process, I set aside several class periods for oral peer response for each paper students wrote. I made sure that each responding group consisted of no fewer than three students to eliminate the effect of a single unhelpful responder, and no more than five students, to assure everyone a chance to read his or her work. In order to model effective commenting, I responded aloud in the beginning to students who volunteered to read their work-in-progress in front of the class. Shortly before papers were due, I distributed handouts of common errors, stocked the classroom with grammar books and dictionaries, made up editing sheets, and allowed time for written peer response.

Finally, when papers were handed in, instead of spending time deciding on and rationalizing grades, I questioned what was not clear, reinforced what I had taught, and responded to what resonated for me. My focus shifted from What is this paper worth? to How can this paper be improved?

At the same time, I jotted down common problems and examples of good writing. On September 25, notations for my fifth-period class looked like this:

- not able to organize comparisons — James
- changes tenses within paragraphs — John
- organized well around theme of Gatsby as magician — Mike
- needs to combine and vary sentences — David M.

- should eliminate repetition — Meri
- needs to expand and develop paragraphs — Matt
- fully developed analysis of *The Awakening* around the theme of suicide — Heather
- doesn't understand noun/pronoun agreement — Tamisha
- needs to rework opening paragraph to make it more inclusive — Michelle
- doesn't maintain tone in conclusion — Brendan
- needs to learn to support generalizations with specifics — Nicole
- problem with passive voice — Laura

These notes became the basis for minilessons. Fifth-period students were attentive, since the lessons were built around their own papers.

For my own record keeping, I recorded brief comments about each student's paper in two squares in my roll book instead of grades. Examples of these comments on the first assignment in September, under the column "summer reading," looked like this:

MIKE: Excellent possibilities with magician image in *Gatsby*. Too much repetition of "I like," but well-organized and fluent.

JOHN: Less than 1/2 typed page of superficial retelling of plot.

ARNAB: No paragraphs. Sounds like the Cliff notes on "Othello." Long and involved, but with no framework or voice.

NICOLE: An enthusiastic reading of *Madame Bovary*, but without focus. Ideas too general and abstract. Needs to be more specific.

Glancing back, I found these hastily written comments more exact for teaching purposes than grades. In the past, sometimes just a few weeks after I had given a C, for example, I had found it hard to remember if it was because the student had only a superficial understanding of the text or because he had difficulty organizing his essay. With this new system, I was better able to observe progress from paper to paper — even if the next assignment was of a different genre, as was this autobiographical essay assigned to the same students:

150

MIKE: Consistent tone. Detailed story about Digger, a friend who almost became a member of the family. Speaks of friend's need but doesn't yet state why Digger was important to him.

JOHN: 2½ pages—more fluent than first paper, but serious writing problems for this level, particularly sentence fragments. Expresses ideas tentatively, even about someone he knows well.

ARNAB: Thoughtful account of affect of TM on his school problems. Clearer and more to the point than first paper. Aware of weaknesses and working on not obfuscating his ideas.

NICOLE: Delicate description of mother. Compares her to a crystal cup with a strong handle; actually, her mother's teacup. Needs to make other details and descriptions more precise.

When I returned their papers, I asked students who had strengths in particular areas to read aloud. Listening to these "published" papers, the class could *hear* ways of improving their work, instead of just *seeing* my written comments.

Throughout the marking period, I also instituted what we came to call "portfolio days." On these days, students selected what they wanted to include in their portfolios and worked on their revisions. Students wrote, peer conferenced in designated corners of the room, or discussed their work with me.

Portfolio days allowed me to work personally with students without giving up my preparation or lunch periods as I had done in the past. They also provided time for me to get to know students individually; to clarify my written comments; to listen to students discuss their own writing processes, fears, and breakthroughs; and to recommend further reading. In a typical fifteen-minute span of miniconferences, Rob asked me why I thought his writing was too general; Diane asked if she could choose a totally different topic for her portfolio piece, since she realized, after hearing her classmates' papers, that she didn't know enough about her subject; and Christine requested models for effective dialogue.

In addition to selecting which papers went into their portfolios, students were required to write an introductory essay. This essay served as a place to reflect on their strengths and weaknesses, their writing styles and habits, and what they had discovered or still wanted to learn. To me, these reflective essays were central to the learning process. Encouraging students to reflect on their writing, I found that they began to think of themselves more as writers. Writing papers was not merely a game to win a grade. Writing was becoming their responsibility.

Other teachers asked, "Isn't using portfolios extra work?" I had to admit that there was planning involved and the portfolios to read, in addition to responding to drafts. But, when it came time to assess the portfolios, because I had seen most of the papers previously, I could read through them and grade holistically. According to my philosophy, adapted from the work of Nancy Sommers (May, 1992) it was unnecessary to respond in detail. Portfolios included finished work. If students wanted a particular response, they could ask me in their introduction.

"What papers should I put into my portfolio?" "How many?" "How will you grade?" My students were anxious; they wanted to know. Depending on the level of the class, I asked for either two or three papers for the final portfolio. What we were studying determined the form. The purpose of this requirement was to make sure that students became competent in forms other than those that they had already practiced. Some students were comfortable with expository essays but had little practice in writing anything more personal. Others had avoided learning more than the most elementary expository formula. As I have repeated throughout this book, growth among my students was uneven. Measuring progress by the portfolio method was a more equitable way to assess a wide range of students.

One of the entries in their portfolios, though, always remained free choice: a piece of writing from our class, from another class, or one done outside of school. Selections varied from a piece we had conferenced on several times to an essay written to attain Eagle Scout status to an argument turned in for history to a poem that had never before left the bureau drawer. But as diverse as portfolios were, they were all the result of engagement and hard work. Students were encouraged to continue to revise selections and include them in future portfolios. They were also encouraged to change forms; for example, to alter a topic they had expressed in an essay to fit within the conventions of a poem.

In assessing portfolios, I chose to consider the amount of effort that went into them, as well as the actual quality of work accomplished. The reason this decision proved a sound one was that it encouraged students to exert themselves—not only those with low skills, but also those who had never before put much effort into English. I asked students to attach their drafts and any written comments they had received with their final papers. And even though I only looked through all this if I wanted to discover how a particular problem had occurred, the students were fastidious. They would direct me to their drafts by using colored paper clips and other clever devices to catch my eye.

A Word About Grading

After eleven years of teaching in a public high school, when I made the decision not to grade writing until the end of the marking period, I considered that I might be taking a risk. My greatest fear was that students would not work unless there were consequences (i.e., grades). Since I had never given my classes an opportunity to write in an atmosphere where grades didn't matter, I assumed that students with an I-don't-care attitude might not work at all.

The opposite occurred. On workshop days, most of my students were prepared and serious about their writing. Organizing themselves, they moved around the room to get the help they needed. And although I kept waiting, only two students mentioned grades. After I showed them my recorded comments, both were satisfied. Mostly, students discussed their work-in-progress. This was particularly true for less skillful writers. No longer hiding behind a blasé attitude, they began to ask questions and to pay closer attention to their classmates' papers. One of my less-able students even called me at home: "Have you read my paper yet? What do you think?" My classroom became a more comfortable place for me and for my students than it had been in the past. Everyone seemed to appreciate "the right to begin again" without penalty.

My second-greatest fear had been the reaction of the administration. If I did not have enough grades in my gradebook when a parent called or a student's performance was questioned, I could be considered an irresponsible teacher. To keep this from happening, I gave quizzes and in-class essay tests to make sure that students read the work I assigned and understood our discussions.

If students did the work, my method of grading actually turned out to be in their favor. Not only did they have an opportunity to get a series of comments from me and their peers, but they also had most of a marking period to upgrade their writing. Unfortunately, this caused a problem: my grades turned out to be higher than those of teachers who were working in more traditional ways. My department head pointed this out to me, as did a colleague who was teaching the same course — without portfolios — across the hall. My comment was this, "If students are given the opportunity to revise and reflect, their writing will improve and so will their grades."

Writing About Writing

Recognition of many sorts resulted from the metacognitive nature of the reflective essays that my students wrote to introduce their portfolios. In the act of writing about writing, they gained awareness, began to question, and even felt confident enough to experiment. Jean, a shy senior who rarely spoke, became more aware of her own writing process. Instead of drafting on paper, Jean spent many hours writing in her head.

In order to get focused, I must brainstorm a few lists first and then concentrate in a quiet spot like my bed. For my still analysis paper, I even had to drive down to the canal, where I sat beside the water in the woods and calmly put my thoughts together. The first draft always takes the longest time. . . .

In the reflective essay that introduced her second portfolio, Jean, now more aware of her writing process, realized some of the limitations she put on herself because of her behavior.

The other problem that I had limiting myself with the sonnet that is also representative of all my writings is that I am too reluctant to stray from my first draft once it is written. With the sonnet, I spent many hours trying new ideas, but I was afraid to start over from scratch if something wasn't working. . . .

Jean began to realize that the length of time she spent drafting in her head contributed to her hesitancy about making changes. In the future, she might not be so "afraid to start over from scratch if something wasn't working." More aware, Jean was preparing herself to watch out for pitfalls.

Laura, a vivacious girl with a strong streak of originality, demonstrated her awareness by asking questions. In her first portfolio, she questioned me. Laura was unsure about standards and also about the five paragraph essay with its three body paragraphs labeled "Bing," "Bang," and "Bongo" in the STEPS format she had studied previously.

One question that I have about my writing is this: would an A paper graded by you be the kind of paper a college student would write? I also get confused about the different types of papers. My older sister in college said that when she writes there is no Bing, Bang and Bongo. I want to know what is going to be expected of me in college writing and if the work we're doing now relates to it.

Laura's concerns were real, and given the hectic nature of the high school environment, she might not have had the opportunity to resolve them. In her second portfolio, though,

Laura began to question even more deeply, challenging the educational process itself:

> I really wish that high school was organized differently. Having to study so many different subjects makes it hard to focus on one class. I think if I could devote myself to writing and studying it that I would produce better quality. Of course that is impossible but this is the class I spend the most time in because it takes more than just putting words together. . . .

Paul, a classmate of Laura's who played on the soccer team, found his portfolio to be a place in which to experiment.

> I think keeping a portfolio is a great idea. I've been able to keep track of my writing, to see if I'm improving, or if I have different voices when I do different types of writing. I spent a lot of time on my portfolio, at least 20 hours total, with the most time being spent on "The Graduate" paper and my Eagle Scout Service Project Proposal.
>
> In the area of improvement and experimentation, I'm trying to write with a more academic voice, to get ready to write knockout college application essays. There seems to be a little progress in each writing that I do, and I hope it will continue to get better. My most prevalent strength is that I am able to interpret into thought what the author, like Goethe, or director, like Nichols, is trying to say, but I run into difficulty when I try to write out my thoughts.
>
> In the writings for the next quarter, I hope to write more descriptive interpretations and be able to be understood without a doubt in the reader's mind. Since I am also on the staff of The Viking Press [our high school newspaper], I hope to do some experimentation by writing about something I do not know much about, which will make me explain the topic more thoroughly, since I won't understand it myself. . . .

Paul might have felt a little too powerful, thinking he could interpret what an author or director was *trying* to say. But it was evident that Paul was becoming strong enough to look at his own writing more critically, remarking on his different "voices." Although I questioned the use of "a more academic voice" to "write knockout college application essays," I was pleased that Paul had begun to experiment with language. Judging by what he told me about his activities with the *Viking Press*, Paul was beginning to feel more like a writer.

Opening a Dialogue

Portfolios, though, didn't work for everyone. Even so, having the opportunity to read a student's opening essay often helped me to begin a dialogue with him. Take Mike's reflective essay, for instance:

> I have included a report and two poems for my portfolio. I chose these three things for one of two reasons: either it was (1) of the best examples of my truly pathetic writing skills, or (2) the piece included all of my heart and feelings at the time.
>
> You will recognize the two pieces that fall under the first catagory and probably kill slaughter and maim them again because I am a bad writer. The other one is something that I had to recall from a folder that is about four year old.
>
> Due to my incredible laziness, poor planning and stupidity I did not have enough time to rewirte the essay on the person that was special to me. don't bother commenting on it because it has all the same errors in it. How ever I was able to redo the sonnet and i would greatly appreciate you comments on it. I would also be grateful if you would comment on my freewriting piece, but please do it on a separate piece of paper because i don't have another copy of this.
>
> Thank you for reading all this garbage and please be nice to me when you grade
>
> Your honest buddy
> Mike

Reading Mike's essay, I realized that Mike saw even my nonjudgmental comments on his writing as attempts to "kill slaughter and maim" him and as evidence that he was a "bad writer." The only piece of writing that had been important to him in over three years of high school had been an in-class freewriting on which there were no teacher comments.

Whether is was due to "incredible laziness, poor planning and stupidity," or whether it was due to Mike's own stage of development, he resisted revising his work. Nevertheless, his reflective essay gave me the opportunity to begin a dialogue with him about this.

"How did you like my freewriting?" Mike wanted to know.

"It was okay for a freshman," I answered. "Why do you want comments on it now? I thought you didn't like comments on your writing."

Mike shrugged. "I'm a terrible writer."

"I think you're pretty good," I told him honestly. "I really enjoyed your reflective essay. The writing is natural and lively, and you have a nice sense of humor. Someone's got to be pretty lucky, though, to get his writing just right the first time. I feel as though I'm depleting a forest, the number of pages I have to revise writing my book."

"You can be pretty bad, Mrs. Lott," Mike joked.

I smiled back. Having taught Mike's overachieving older brothers and sisters in previous years, I understood his laid-back attitude, even though it bordered on carelessness. Mike was the baby of the family, satisfied with his own spontaneity and afraid to be judged in the adult world. I suppose Mike thought that if he really tried, he might fall short. As his teacher, I wanted to keep our dialogue open. Mike's introduction allowed me to do so.

Tom, on the other hand, used his reflective essay to begin a dialogue with me. Tom was not only angry about my comments on his paper, but he was also unhappy with my assignments.

Dear Mrs. Lott,

[The] words written by you on my essay "Who has meant the most to me," . . . cut through me like a knife. I've never had a teacher who hasn't enjoyed my writing or given me nothing but an A. In my essay I put a lot of time into bringing out the emotions I wanted to convey to you. My heart bled and there were tears in my eyes when I was through. I put all the love I feel for my Father in that essay. Then you gave it back to me [with your comments]. Now that I look back I couldn't agree with you more. At the time however I was crushed. I don't show my pain through sorrow. I show it through anger. I was cursing you out left and right (not to your face of course). I wanted nothing more at that moment [than] to quit your class. If I did I feel it would have been the greatest mistake of my life. You showed me that even though there was emotion and love in it, I needed more. I needed to take that love and organize it. I needed to follow the correct forms of English. For this I thank you.

Even though you showed me what I need to do I just can't. I did not put that particular essay in my portfolio. My emotions are to [sic] damn jumbled to [put] on paper right now. I really hope I can work on that.

My sonnet has been included in my portfolio. Now you're probably saying. "Tom, that was a very well organized piece. You put raw emotion on paper and you followed the rules." That last word is the key. Rules. I can put things on paper when there are rules and limitations. Such as the case with my political philosophy. There was emotion involved but there were rules I had to follow. That is why I feel it is well written.

If I can ask of you one favor it would be to give us an assignment w[h]ere we need to put raw emotion on paper. There are a million great emotions and thoughts in my head and I want to share them with the rest of the world. If you could do this for me I would be eternally grateful.

Sincerely,
Thomas J. Smith III

I was experienced enough to know that I could not elicit eternal gratitude from Tom, but I did try to clarify my intentions. When I returned his portfolio, I enclosed a letter to him apologizing for any comments that might have been hurtful on his essay about his father. In my letter, I also told him that love, by its very nature, is not organized, and that I did not know of a "correct form of English" in which love should be expressed. I encouraged Tom to continue to work on this essay for his next portfolio if he could. I also told him that, as

159

writers, we discover the form that works for us and for our audience, but often not until we have sufficient time and distance to do that. In answer to Tom's request for an assignment allowing him "to put raw emotion on paper," I invited him to give it a try. After all, portfolios are a place in which to take risks.

Portfolios, with their accompanying reflective essays, allow students to act as writers. In the process of compiling portfolios and reflecting on their work, students have the opportunity to learn even more than they did in the initial writing process. And, by reading student portfolios, teachers can learn more about their students.

Conclusion

*S*ince I had never written a book, I did not know what my experience was going to be. Some of my friends had written books. I had, of course, read books. But writing my own book was like riding a two-wheeler without my father's hand on the seat, or taking the bus to New York City for the first time, or having my first child. While writing *A Teacher's Stories*, I traveled from what I knew into what I did not know.

I knew what my circumstances had been in the classroom. At South Brunswick High School, my experience had been a text that I had lived but of which I had not yet made sense. I wrote in my journal on May 31, when I was almost halfway through this book:

> It's almost as though we see our work in fragments—this paper; that paper, forty minutes here; fifteen minutes there. I used to complain that teaching was not like building cabinets. I never got to see the finished product. Writing about teaching, though, has helped complete this experience for me. I don't see cabinets, but I do see chapters.

Writing was the way I made sense of my experience.

I was aware, however, that there were limitations to my stories. I fantasized about printing chapters without endings, so that other teachers could add their own. And though I tried to be open minded in my reflections, I knew there were conflicts of interest. My own critical analysis was limited. Can an author be narrator and critic at the same time?

All this I knew. What I did not know was who I had become, how things were going to change, and what I was going to do. Melanie Sperling of Stanford University, in a talk she gave at the 1991 NCTE conference in Seattle, spoke about the stories that her student teachers had written. Sperling referred to these stories as "reflective mirrors." As I wrote my narratives, I found myself looking into a reflective mirror, unsure of who I was.

The spring of my sabbatical, while I was working on my book, I wrote the following journal entries, to try to understand my confusion:

March 29: I still care about teaching, yet I am no longer sure of my role as a teacher. Thursday when I went to school to pick up my mail Priya spotted me and asked me to come in and hear the essays they were reading aloud in C102. I listened, while I watched my former students playing with silly putty and peering at the clock. They were reading "form" essays — "advanced persuasive," Carol called them. Carol seemed pleased; the students had followed her assignment. Fitting back in is going to be a big problem for me in September.

May 15: I'm planning to go to school today to pick up my mail. Such ambivalent feelings. It seems as though it takes so long a journey to get there. Seeing so many English teachers all at once — feeling their frustration and pain. No wonder Tom and the others who have retired from our department never came back. "I'll be back," they said. But we never saw them.

June 7: Is there a situation other than teaching where a person deals intimately, on a daily basis, with so many people? Funny, now that I know how complex and sensitive teaching is, I am not sure I can go back to a situation where teaching "the right way," without killing myself, is impossible.

Writing my way into unknown territory, I found myself questioning whether I wanted to teach and whether or not I wanted to remain at my job.

I began to wish for something more than a teacher's job the way it existed. I wished that high school English teachers had enough time to consider individual differences, that class sizes and class loads were smaller than they are. With each class containing twenty-six seventeen and eighteen-year-olds, I find it impossible to carefully listen to all my students and consider their various backgrounds no matter how hard I try. With a teaching load of five periods, I cannot reflect on each student's progress and respond to the continuous stacks of papers that accumulate on my desk. And I know that the professional lives of my colleagues all over the world are in many cases more frustrating than mine.

Ultimately, I wished that more high school teachers would be encouraged by their schools to become teacher/researchers. As Richard Bullock (1987) suggests, reduced course loads during research projects, paid leave to reflect on what happened during those projects, and a place where high school teachers can work in solitude would provide starting places. Aware as I am of financial constraints, I cannot think of a better investment for taxpayers. Although money is spent on teacher training and outside consultants, teachers are not often inspired to be active learners. Instead, told what and how to teach by supervisors, parents, curriculum developers, and even textbooks, many teachers either have defensively refused to change or have become confused and frustrated. Strengthened by experiencing my own confusion as a valid response to the complexities of teaching and not as a problem, and by being able to share with my colleagues and students what I have learned, I know that others would profit from the same opportunities. In this way, education can become more vital.

Nancie Atwell (1982) described the effect of teachers doing their own research:

> We have discovered that the teacher who is also a researcher is no longer a victim of "our profession's energy crisis." When we change our role to that of an inquirer, we become learners, too. We no longer feel drained by the demands we impose on ourselves when we view our classrooms as contexts we motivate, orchestrate, and evaluate. Instead, we are energized.

Ultimately, I returned to South Brunswick for some of the same reasons that other English teachers return to their high schools September after September: I like my students, I like my colleagues, I need the money, I have a secure job. Nevertheless, my classes are too large, there are far too many papers to read and comment on every weekend, and there is no individual space in which to work.

Although my own thinking has changed, I do not know how to effect change in the high school itself. Susan Moore Johnson (1990) writes:

> The public-school teachers in this study did participate in decision making, but the majority executed their influence intermittently and informally rather than through systematic and sustained procedures.... An English teacher observed a deep feeling of powerlessness to affect any policy in his suburban school.... Another suburban teacher who was asked whether she felt any sense of power responded, "Powerful? No, I feel drained."

As an English teacher in a public high school, there seem to be few networks through which to make my influence felt beyond my own classroom. As critics of public education have noted, schools remain today as they were designed nearly a century ago, when the rage was the mass-production system and the factory model. In this approach, teachers work on assigned fragments, with little say in overall design.

Like the teachers interviewed by Susan Moore Johnson, "I feel drained." Education can only improve if teachers are empowered. Yet, as the nineties progress, I see more emphasis on management and evaluation, resulting in the dampening of teachers' initial enthusiasm.

I am uncertain of how to become a better teacher in public education. I do not know how to work effectively in a system that has so many levels of supervision, so much compartmentalization, and so many job classifications. I am saddened that teachers are sometimes rewarded for becoming passive rather than active participants.

As a writer, however, I feel more optimistic. In the past, I have discovered while writing what was important to me and what I needed to know. Together, as teachers, we can discover what we need to know, while teaching our students to become writers along with us.

References

Achebe, C. 1986. *Things fall apart*. Portsmouth, NH: Heinemann.

Albee, E. 1983. *Who's afraid of Virginia Woolf?* New York: Atheneum.

Angelou, M. 1980. *I know why the caged bird sings*. New York: Bantam.

Atwell, N. 1982. Class-based writing research: Teachers learning from students. *English Journal* January. Urbana, IL: National Council of Teachers of English.

Berthoff, A. 1987. The teacher as REsearcher. In *Reclaiming the classroom*, edited by D. Goswami & P. Stillman. Portsmouth, NH: Boynton/Cook.

Bissex, G. & R. H. Bullock, eds. 1987. *Seeing for ourselves*. Portsmouth, NH: Heinemann.

Bullock, R. H. 1987. A quiet revolution: The power of teacher research. In *Seeing for ourselves*, edited by G. Bissex and R. H. Bullock. Portsmouth, NH: Heinemann.

Carlson, G., ed. 1973. *Western literature*. New York: McGraw-Hill.

Chopin, K. 1981. *The awakening*. New York: Modern Library.

Christensen, C. R. 1989. *Teaching and the case method*. Boston: Harvard Business School.

Chute, C. 1985. *The Beanes of Egypt, Maine*. New York: Warner.

Coles, R. 1989. *The call of stories*. Boston: Houghton Mifflin.

Elbow, P. 1986. *Embracing contraries*. New York: Oxford University Press.

Goswami, D. & P. Stillman, eds. 1987. *Reclaiming the classroom*. Portsmouth, NH: Boynton/Cook.

Gottlieb, D. 1991. *Family matters*. New York: E. P. Dutton.

Graves, D. 1978. We can end the energy crisis. *Language Arts* 55:795-96.

Hanley, W. *Slow dance on the killing ground*. New York: Dramatists Play Service.

Hansen, A. J. 1989. In *Teaching and the case method* by C. R. Christensen with A. J. Hansen. Boston: Harvard Business School.

Hesse, H. *Siddhartha*. New York: New Directions.

Holt, J. 1964. *How children fail*. New York: Delacorte.

Johnson, S. 1990. *Teachers at work*. New York: Basic.

Kafka, F. 1988. *The metamorphosis*. New York: Bantam.

Lott, J. G. 1991. Jeremy: Sex, lies, and masks. *English Journal* March. Urbana, IL: National Council of Teachers of English.

Nelms, B. 1991. The case of the recalcitrant student: A teacher at work. *English Journal* March. Urbana, IL: National Council of Teachers of English.

Newkirk, T., ed. 1985. *To compose*. 2nd ed. Portsmouth, NH: Heinemann.

Nicolaides, K. 1969. *The natural way to draw*. New York: Houghton Mifflin.

Prentice Hall Literature: World Masterpieces. 1991. Englewood Cliffs, NJ: Prentice Hall.

Root, R. L. Jr. 1991a. In *Writer's craft, teacher's art*, edited by M. Schwartz. Portsmouth, NH: Boynton/Cook.

———. 1991b. The Virgule variations: Learning/Language/Literature. *English Journal* October. Urbana, IL: National Council of Teachers of English.

Rose, M. 1989. *Lives on the boundary*. New York: Free Press.

Salinger, J. D. 1951. *Catcher in the rye*. New York: Bantam.

Schwartz, M., ed. 1991. *Writer's craft, teacher's art*. Portsmouth, NH: Boynton/Cook.

Shakespeare, W. 1958. *A midsummer night's dream*. New York: Simon & Schuster.

Shelley, M. 1981. *Frankenstein*. New York: Bantam.

Sommers, N. 1982. Responding to student writing. *College Composition and Communication* May:148-56.

Tannen, D. 1990. *You just don't understand*. New York: Ballentine.

Wacht, F. 1986. *I remember: An autobiography text for high school students*. Littletown, MA: Copley.

Williams, T. 1947. *A streetcar named Desire*. New York: Singer.

———. 1970. *The glass menagerie*. New York: New Directions.

Yount, D. & P. De Kock. 1979. *Steps*. Lakeside, CA: Interact.

Zinnser, W. 1988. *Writing to learn*. New York: HarperCollins.

Credits

Throughout the years, I have been influenced by many writers. I wish to thank the following proprietors for permission to quote copyrighted works:

Nancie Atwell from "Class-Based Writing Research: Teachers Learning from Students," *English Journal.* Copyright © January 1982 by the National Council of Teachers of English. Reprinted by permission.

Ann E. Berthoff from *Reclaiming the Classroom,* edited by Dixie Goswami and Peter R. Stillman. (Boynton/Cook Publishers, Inc., Portsmouth, NH, 1987.) Reprinted by permission.

Robert Coles from *The Call of Stories.* Houghton Mifflin Co., 1989. Reprinted by permission of the publisher.

Daniel Gottlieb from *Family Matters.* Penguin USA, 1991. Reprinted by permission of the publisher.

Abby J. Hansen from "Suggestions for Seminar Participants" in C. Roland Christensen with Abby J. Hansen, *Teaching and the Case Method.* Boston: Harvard Business School, 1989. Reprinted by permission of the publisher.

John Holt from *How Children Fail.* Delacorte Press, a Division of Bantam, Doubleday, Dell Publishing Group, Inc., 1964. Reprinted by permission of the publisher.

Susan Moore Johnson from *Teachers at Work, Achieving Success in Our Schools.* Basic Books, 1990. Reprinted by permission of the publisher.

Joyce Greenberg Lott from "Jeremy: Sex, Lies, and Masks," *English Journal* Copyright © March 1991 by the National Council of Teachers of English. Reprinted by permission.